CHRIST IN THE
LEVITICAL OFFERINGS

CHRIST IN THE LEVITICAL OFFERINGS

J M Flanigan

JOHN RITCHIE LTD
CHRISTIAN PUBLICATIONS

40 Beansburn, Kilmarnock, Scotland

ISBN-13: 978 1 907731 26 6

Copyright © 2011 by John Ritchie Ltd.
40 Beansburn, Kilmarnock, Scotland

Typeset by John Ritchie Ltd., Kilmarnock
Printed by Bell & Bain Ltd., Glasgow

Contents

Preface

The value and efficacy of the atoning work of the Lord Jesus at Calvary is such, that no human mind, having come into the good of redemption, can fully appreciate it nor give expression to it. And yet there is no doubt that a thoughtful consideration of the five major Offerings is of immense help in aiding an understanding and appreciation of a work which has brought multitudes into a sphere of unparalleled blessing. It would seem that a meditative study of the "Types and Shadows" has now largely lost its appeal, with the resulting impoverishment, not only of individual believers but also their collective gatherings. The reader of this publication will warm to its content as step by step one is meticulously led through the holy requirements so necessary in preserving the typical significance of the important issues being presented.

This latest work from our highly respected brother in Christ bears the imprint of his thoughtful and spiritually sensitive method of communicating his understanding and appreciation of the subject before him. Not only has the varied aspects of the major Offerings been ably dealt with but also (dare I suggest a bonus) included are what our brother Jim refers to as "subsidiary" Offerings. While these are not so often expounded in detail and perhaps even less often included in a written work they form an ideal appendage to the main focus of the book, confirming to the reader: "That beginning at Moses and all the prophets, He expounded unto them in all the Scriptures, the things concerning Himself"; Luke ch.24 v27.

It has been an uplifting experience for me to have had the privilege to read and peruse the pages of this succinct but God honouring consideration of the One expressed in the words of the hymn; "No subject so glorious as He, No theme so exulting to us".

E. Taylor

Introduction

The Purpose of the Offerings

It is not difficult to find Christ in the Levitical Offerings for the Offerings are ancient foreshadowings of Himself, ancient indeed, for they were cast some fifteen hundred years before the Saviour came. In typical language they portray the glory of His Person, the beauty of His character and the greatness of His work. They show His people His inestimable preciousness to God both in the loveliness of His life and in the value of His sacrifice, and they describe in detail the privilege of believers of approach to God in the holy exercises of supplication and worship. They are a spiritual mine, a virtual treasury of divine revelation, perhaps especially as touching the Son of God in His suffering and death.

No one who has found Christ in the Offerings has ever regretted the study of those portions of God's Word where the Offerings are outlined. With some saints the only regret may be that the treasure was not discovered earlier in life. It is hoped that these meditations may encourage some believers to commence a study of the Offerings even now, and that those who are already in the enjoyment of them may yet discover fresh beauties of the Lord Jesus, God's Son and our Saviour.

Authority for finding Christ here

If anyone should ask for authority for so finding Christ in these ancient Offerings, there is certainly no lack of such authority. The Lord Jesus Himself, walking to Emmaus with two of His disciples, showed that privileged couple that there were things concerning Himself in all the Scriptures. He was in the writings of Moses and of the prophets and He was in the Psalms too (Luke ch 24.v 27, v 44). In the New Testament the writer to the

Hebrews refers much to types of the Person and work of Christ in the Tabernacle and Offerings (Heb.ch 8.vv 1-5; ch 9. vv 1-9; ch 10 .vv 1-9). These were patterns he says, they were figures of the true, they were shadows, as has been noted, of which our Lord Jesus is the fulfilment and substance. In light of this, how sad, indeed how tragic, that anyone should dismiss the Book of Leviticus with its story of the Offerings as but a record of old Jewish rites and rituals of no importance to New Testament believers.

The Principal Offerings

There are five principal Offerings presented in the early chapters of Leviticus. They are, the Burnt Offering, the Meat Offering, the Peace Offering, the Sin Offering and the Trespass Offering. It must be emphasised however that these are but the principal Offerings. There are other subsidiary or auxiliary Offerings such as the Drink Offering, where a small quantity of wine was poured on the Offering, (Exod. ch 29 v:40; Lev.ch 23: v 18; Num. ch 15:vv 5,7). Then there is the lesser known Wood Offering, mentioned only by Nehemiah (ch 10.v 34, ch13. v31), and so necessary for the maintenance of the fire upon the altar, which was never to go out (Lev.ch 6.vv 12-13).

The principal Offerings are first mentioned in a most significant order. In first place was the Burnt Offering, and we shall see how rightly this Offering should have that place. Second is the Meat Offering, so closely associated with the Burnt Offering and invariably seen as a companion to it. In central place there is the Peace Offering and it will become beautifully obvious that such indeed is the rightful place of this fellowship Offering. These are followed by the Sin Offering and the Trespass Offering and since both of these are so directly concerned with sin they are at times joined together and referred to as the Guilt Offerings.

Why such a Variety of Offerings?

Should the question arise as to why such a variety of Offerings was necessary, the question may well be answered with another question, "Why four Gospels in the New Testament?" The reason for both is the excelling greatness of Christ. Such is the wonder of His Person that He must be viewed from several different aspects if one is to have any intelligent appreciation of that greatness. It is rather like an accomplished architect or builder surveying a building. Such must view the building from all aspects, from the East, the West, the North and the South since beauties observable from one aspect may not necessarily be seen from another. To gain a full-orbed picture the building must be viewed from every aspect and only then will the architectural beauty be fully appreciated. So Matthew, Mark, Luke and John all present Christ in different ways. He is always the same glorious Person but that glory shines variously like the several facets of a diamond. Four Gospels are necessary to portray His varied glories to us and likewise several Offerings are necessary to help men to a fuller appreciation of His Person. The necessity for four Gospels and several Offerings but emphasises the glory and majesty of the Son of God in His incomparable worth and work. May we, as we read, indeed find Christ in the Levitical Offerings.

The Priesthood

It is perhaps fitting that brief mention should be made here of the importance of the priesthood, for so much of what follows was indeed dependent upon priestly ministry. For instance, there was no Sin Offering until the inauguration of the priesthood. Offerings prior to that were approach Offerings or Burnt Offerings, by which men acknowledged their need of forgiveness for approach to God. Today, natural men cannot draw near, neither in worship nor in what many are pleased to call "divine service". Such are aspects of priestly ministry and the natural man is not a priest. This belongs to those who are linked with the Saviour, our Great High Priest. He has made His people a Kingdom of priests (Rev 1.6) and engagement in the service of the sanctuary is a priestly privilege.

A consideration of the Levitical Offerings will reveal just how essential the priest was and apart from Offerings he had a multitude of other duties. Men were dependant on him for so much. They looked up to him to be guided by him, and to be comforted by him in days of darkness and trouble. When the foul disease of leprosy afflicted them it was to the priest that they turned for direction as to what to do.

In these meditations we are concerned with the priests' role in the various Levitical and associated Offerings. In a later chapter a more detailed consideration will be given to the solemn consecration of the priests.

Leviticus ch 1. vv 1-17; ch 6. vv 8-13

Christ in the Burnt Offering

Leviticus and the Divine Call

The name "Leviticus" indicates that this third book of the Pentateuch has to do chiefly with the service of the Levites. Adam Clarke however, helpfully enlarges on this and writes, "The Greek version of the Septuagint, and the Vulgate Latin, have given the title of Leviticus to the third book of the Pentateuch, and the name has been retained in almost all the modern versions. The book was thus called because it treats principally of the laws and regulations of the Levites and priests in general. In Hebrew it is termed *arqyw Vaiyikra*, meaning, "And he called," which is the first word in the book".

Leviticus begins then with the call of God to Moses but this was not the first time that Moses had heard the divine call. In Exodus ch 3 v .4 "God called unto him out of the midst of the bush, and said, Moses, Moses. And he said, Here am I". Again, in Exodus ch 19.v 3 "Moses went up unto God, and the Lord called unto him out of the mountain". Now, in that interesting prelude to the Book of Leviticus in Exodus ch 40.vv 34-35, the tabernacle has been set up and "the glory of the LORD filled the tabernacle. And Moses was not able to enter into the tent of the congregation, because the cloud abode thereon, and the glory of the LORD filled the tabernacle". It is then that Leviticus begins, saying, "And the LORD called unto Moses, and spake unto him out of the tabernacle of the congregation".

Three times then, Moses hears the call of God, out of the bush, out of the mountain, and out of the glory-filled

12

tabernacle. It may be said that the call from the bush was a call to service, he was being chosen and commissioned to lead the people. The call from the mountain, associated with the giving of the law, was a call to holiness, and the call from out of the tabernacle was a call to worship. Matthew Henry remarks, "The moral law was given with terror from a burning mountain in thunder and lightning; but the remedial law of sacrifice was given more gently from a mercy-seat, because that was typical of the grace of the gospel, which is the ministration of life and peace".

Detailed Instructions

There now follows in chapter 1, detailed instructions regarding the Burnt Offering. There had of course been Burnt Offerings before the giving of the law, as, for example, in the case of Job (Job ch 1.v 5), Noah (Gen ch 8.v 20), Abraham (Gen ch 22.vv 3,6,7,8,13). Those however, were the exercise of individuals personally desiring to bring some Offering to Jehovah. Now there were to be directions nationally concerning priesthood and Offerings, and as has been mentioned earlier, the Burnt Offering has first place.

"If any man of you bring an Offering unto the LORD". The word here translated "bring" is not quite as simple as appears on a first reading. B.W. Newton explains, "The word, which in our version is rendered "bring" means to present as an offering. It implies, in its Levitical use, solemnity of presentation".

Perhaps there is an instance of divine grace here, even under law. The word "man" is the Hebrew *Adam*, (Strong 120) man of the dust, creature of the clay. "LORD" is the great Name "Jehovah" (Strong 3068) the eternal, omnipotent, omniscient, self sufficient One. What a privilege is this, that puny man should be permitted, indeed invited, to offer something to the Almighty. This privilege is still the portion of God's people today, and in our worship, in a fuller, greater way, we bring to Jehovah our appreciation of Christ, the great fulfilment and antitype of every Offering.

Variety of Burnt Offerings

Once again grace shines through. If a man was able he should bring a bullock from his herd, but Jehovah recognises that not everyone had such resources and in such cases a man might bring a sheep or a goat. But some could not rise even to that and then a man might bring his Offering from the fowls, whether turtle-doves or young pigeons. Every Offering however, was indeed a shadow of the Christ who was to come. Like the bullock He would be the strong, patient unwearying Servant of Jehovah. As Newberry writes, "The bullock ploughed the land, brought home the sheaves from the harvest field, trod out the corn for the family – type of Him who was the pattern Evangelist, Pastor, and Teacher". What a delight for us to bring to the Father our appreciation of such a Servant, He of whom it was predicted, and fulfilled, "He shall not fail" (Isaiah ch 42.v 4). It is not surprising that Jehovah should say, "Behold my Servant" (Isaiah ch 42.v 1). The offering must be a male, symbolic of strength, initiative, activity and responsibility. So, our Lord Jesus did not live a monastic, cloistered life, hidden away from the bustle of the noisy world around. He was active, a Man among men, living in the midst of defilement but Himself remaining undefiled as we shall see,

Then of course, a man could not have known in those days that if he brought a sheep he was offering a foregleam of the meek and gentle Lamb of God who would, without a murmur, be led as a Lamb to the slaughter to suffer at dark Calvary.

The turtle-doves and pigeons would be a fitting type of Him who lived, and died, in poverty, of whom Paul would later write, "Ye know His poverty ... He became poor" (2 Cor ch 8.v 9). Every Offering, whether from the herd, from the flock, or from the fowls, was, in some way, a foreshadowing of Christ.

Without Blemish

The bullock, as indeed all the Offerings, must be "without blemish". How often this is emphasised throughout. Only such an unblemished Offering would be a fitting type of Him of whom it would be written, "The precious blood of Christ, as of a Lamb without blemish and without spot" (1 Peter ch 1.v 19). He was sinlessly perfect, perfectly sinless, in thought, word and deed.

The offerer must then bring his offering to the door of the tabernacle, and on this point Matthew Henry deserves to be quoted again. He writes, "It must be offered at the door of the tabernacle, where the brazen altar of burnt-offerings stood, which sanctified the gift, and not elsewhere. He must offer it at the door, as one unworthy to enter, and acknowledging that there is no admission for a sinner into covenant and communion with God, but by sacrifice".

Acceptance
He will offer the bullock "for his acceptance". This is agreed by most Hebrew scholars to be more accurate than "of his own voluntary will" as in the K.J.V (v.3). The offerer would be accepted in all the acceptability of his offering. So is the believer today "accepted in the beloved" (Eph ch 1. v 6) and His acceptance is the measure of ours. How important to remember too, that there is no progress in acceptance, neither are there any grades or degrees in acceptance. The youngest, simplest believer in Christ is equally and eternally accepted with the oldest and most knowledgeable saint. We may indeed progress in knowledge, and in our appreciation, but not in acceptance.

In the very shadow of the brazen altar a man must now put his hand upon the head of his offering. The meaning is rather that he should lean or press upon the head of the bullock, in which symbolic act all the value and acceptability of his Offering is being imputed to him, and then, in an exceedingly solemn moment "he shall kill the bullock". He himself becomes responsible for the death of the sacrifice in which he is accepted. And so it is with those who believe today. Perhaps John Newton had learned this when he wrote,

*My conscience felt and owned my guilt
And plunged me in despair.
I saw my sins His blood had spilt
And helped to nail Him there.*

And yet it must ever be remembered that when coming in worship to present our gift to God we are not to be occupied with our sins, but with Him who died for us and in whom we have been brought near.

Atonement

The word "atonement" in v.4 must be remarked upon. The man who brought a Burnt Offering did not bring it in connection with any particular sin for which he needed forgiveness. He rather knew that his life had not been faithfully lived for Jehovah's pleasure. He had come short. Approaching God as a worshipper therefore he needed to be covered. Conscious of imperfection and failure he nevertheless desires to draw near in gratitude to give his gift to the Lord. His own life has not been acceptable so he offers another life which will be wholly burnt upon the altar, all for God. We may indeed be sinners but when we come to God as worshippers we are covered in Him who is our Burnt Offering. There are two different Hebrew words for "burn". We shall meet the other word in the Sin Offering, but here the word signifies a burning which causes the offering to rise in a sweet savour, a savour of rest, to the Lord. So is the Burnt Offering often called "the ascending Offering. The Hebrew word is *olah* (Strong 5930) as in "holocaust", rising in smoke.

The Offering Flayed and Offered

There is now a practical problem. Having killed his offering, the offerer must now flay, or skin, the animal. The priests will attend to the blood, sprinkling or casting it upon the sides of the altar, but would every man be capable of skinning a bullock? Perhaps not. A helpful change in the text has been suggested, indicating "he shall have it flayed". The priest, or some suitable Levite, will then have the privilege of assisting others at the altar. How such men are needed today, men who can not only worship but who can, as it were, assist others at the altar, perhaps expressing what other believers would like to say but do not have the ability.

Head, Fat, Inwards and Legs

The Offering must now be cut into its pieces, the head, the fat, the inwards and the legs. When the Lord Jesus expounded the law He summed up the first part by saying, "Thou shalt love the Lord thy God with all thy heart, and with all thy soul, and with all thy mind, and with all thy strength" (Mark ch 12. v 30): Notice how this is in parallel with Leviticus ch1.vv 8,9). The head is the mind; the fat is the soul; the inwards agree with the heart; the strength is the legs. All these parts were placed in order upon the altar fire and burned to ascend in a sweet savour. So was our Lord Jesus entirely devoted to God in perfection. Notice the words "in order". So must our worship be orderly. However brief, it must be intelligent, instructed, sincere devoted approach to God.

Why then, it may be asked, do the inwards and legs need to be "washed in water". The answer is simple. It was not that the Lord Jesus required such cleansing. It was to make the inwards and legs typically what the Saviour was intrinsically. His holy mind, His perfect walk, His inward thoughts and feelings and His strength of character were all pure, completely devoted to the Father.

Sheep and Goats

If the Offering was a sheep or a goat the directions were, in the main, similar to those of the bullock. But while we think of the meekness and gentleness of the sheep, there is a delightful feature in the goat, referred to in Proverbs ch 30.vv29-31, where it is described as "comely in going". The New Translation by JND says, "A stately step". How true this was of Him of whom we sing, "A perfect path of purest grace unblemished and complete". In beautiful dignity and resolute purpose He moved in accord with the will of His Father whatever the cost. His was indeed a stately step.

Turtle Doves or Pigeons

It remains only to remark briefly on the birds. These would not, in the market places of men, have the same value as the bullock or the sheep, but they are equally types or symbols of Him who was precious to God and so are appreciated and accepted by Him. The JFB Commentary is most helpful here and deserves to be quoted in full. "The gentle nature and cleanly habits of the dove led to its selection, while all other fowls were rejected, either for the fierceness of their disposition or the grossness of their taste; and in this case, there being from the smallness of the animal no blood for waste, the priest was directed to prepare it *at* the altar and sprinkle the blood. This was the offering appointed for the poor". The Commentary then adds, "The fowls were always offered in pairs, and the reason why Moses ordered two turtledoves or two young pigeons, was not merely to suit the convenience of the offerer, but according as the latter was in season; for pigeons are sometimes quite hard and unfit for eating, at which time turtledoves are very good in Egypt and Palestine. The turtledoves are not restricted to any age because they are always good when they appear in those countries, being birds of passage; but the age of the pigeons is particularly marked that they might not be offered to God at times when they are rejected by men"

The offerer must bring the birds to the priest and in the shadow of the altar the priest would pinch off the head, burn it on the altar fire and press out all the blood at the side of the altar. While the head burned on the altar the priest would then remove the crop and the feathers. Many expositors are convinced that "feathers" should rather be "dung" or "filth". It may indeed be that which has been collected in the crop but not digested. There is nothing akin to this in Christ and so that which is removed must be cast away, eastward to the place of the ashes.

The body of the bird must then be cleft in the middle with a wing on either side, but it must not be divided asunder. It has been said that a bird cannot be divided into two parts without breaking a bone and this must never be. "A bone of it shall not be broken". So John, a close witness of the Saviour's death at Calvary, records, "They brake not His legs" (John ch 19. v 33)

The bird on the fire of the altar became, just as the bullock, the sheep or the goat, "a burnt sacrifice, an offering made by fire, of a sweet savour unto the LORD".

The Skin of the Offering

While it is often correctly emphasised that the Burnt Offering was wholly for God, yet there was one important exception to this.

In a rather isolated verse in chapter 7 it is stated, "And the priest that offereth any man's Burnt Offering, even the priest shall have to himself the skin of the Burnt Offering which he hath offered" (7.8). Apart from the skin the whole offering was indeed burnt on the altar. It is evident from Leviticus ch 13. vv 47,48, that skins were used to make garments for the people. The lesson here is that the priest, and perhaps the priestly family, were covered by that which had been offered to and accepted by Jehovah. So are we who believe covered with all the acceptability and preciousness of Christ to God. In God's eyes we bear the likeness of His Son, and so should it be practically and morally, in our testimony among men.

Several commentators are of the opinion that this custom of the priest having a right to the skin actually dates from Eden. Adam Clarke comments that "Bishop Patrick supposes that this right of the priest to the skin commenced with the offering of Adam, "for it is probable," says he, "that Adam himself offered the first sacrifice, and had the skin given him by God to make garments for him and his wife; in conformity to which the priests ever after had the skin of the whole burnt-offerings for their portion". Whether this is so or not, it was, in these Levitical days, now a divinely ordained right with a typical meaning.

What an Offering then was this! The unblemished Offering presented to God in its pieces and burnt on the altar fire while the incense ascended to Jehovah as a sweet savour of rest. The offerer stood accepted in his Offering and the priest was covered by the skin of that which had been offered.

Leviticus ch 2. vv1-16; ch 6. vv14-18

Christ in the Meat Offering

Meat or Meal?

Any thoughtful believer coming to a consideration of this Offering for the first time will likely be confronted with two problems. First, those who are familiar with the King James or Authorised Version will know that the Offering is there consistently called "a Meat Offering", but most other versions will differ from this and rather call it a Cereal Offering (RSV), a Grain Offering (NIV), or a Meal Offering (ASV), which latter term is that used by perhaps the majority of preachers and commentators. "Meal Offering" is preferred by these because the substance of the Offering was indeed flour or grain. Strictly speaking however, this is not a translation of the Hebrew word *minchaah* (Strong 4503). This word literally means "a solemn offering or presentation" and is in many other places rendered "present" as in 1 Kings ch 10.v 25, or "gifts" as in 2 Samuel ch 8. v 2, or simply "offering" as in its last occurrence in Malachi ch 3 v.4.

"Meat" therefore is right when used in the sense of a gift of food, just as meat is understood, for instance, in John ch 4. v 34, "My *meat* is to do the will of Him that sent Me". There is no thought of flesh here as there is in the modern usage of the word. "Meal" is correct since the Offering was, in the main, fine flour or meal. So the student must ask, "Meat or Meal?" Helpfully, and perhaps correctly, the JND version avoids both of these terms and simply calls the Offering "an oblation", a gift, the essential meaning of the Hebrew *minchaah*.

A Bloodless Offering?

The second problem may appear to be more serious. Here is

an Offering without blood! A bloodless Offering? Surely many will see this as being at variance with the divine demands. Was not Cain rejected for this very thing, bringing an Offering with no blood? (Gen ch 4). The answer to this difficulty is perhaps two-fold. First, this Offering was not in any sense an Offering for sin. The offerer in this case was simply presenting a gift of gratitude to Jehovah, not for any sin or with any request for forgiveness   Secondly, the Meat Offering was never offered alone. It was an appendage or adjunct to the Burnt Offering or the Peace Offering, so that we may often read of "the Burnt Offering with his Meat Offering", as in Numbers ch 15. v 24; ch 29. v 6; 2 Kings ch 16. v 15. This means therefore that when the flour of the Meat Offering was placed on the altar of Burnt Offering it must have been saturated there with the blood of the Offering which it accompanied. F.H.White says,"There is no instance in Scripture of a Meat Offering being offered by itself. The Jealousy Offering, in connection with which no other sacrifices were offered, was not a true Meat Offering. It was not composed of fine flour, but of rough barley meal. No oil or frankincense was put upon it, for it was a memorial of iniquity" (Num ch 5. v 15).

There is the thought too that these types of the death of Christ in the Burnt Offering and of the lovely life of Christ in the Meat Offering are inseparable. The value of the Saviour's sacrifice is such because of the perfection and moral beauty of His life, and the value of that incomparable life is such because it was eventually poured out in death.

Suffering
While there is no thought of death in this Offering, and no blood-shedding or suffering for sin, or atonement, there are nevertheless typical suggestions of deep suffering and these will be observed in a study of the different forms in which the flour of the Offering was prepared and offered. It was "an Offering made by fire". There was first of all the bruising of the corn which was necessary for the production of fine flour.

Then there was the intense heat of the oven, and the fire associated with the flat plate and the frying pan. Our Lord Jesus had sufferings during His lifetime apart from those which we term "atoning". As believers sing, "Forever on Thy burdened heart a weight of sorrow hung". He was a Man of sorrows who suffered the pangs of being misunderstood, the hurt of misrepresentation, reproach and rejection. He bore the sadness of unbelief even in His own household and family (John ch 7.v 5), and then the final and cruel rejection by the nation to which He had come as the promised Messiah. "He came unto His own and His own received Him not" (John ch 1. v 11). He was indeed a Man of sorrows, acquainted with grief.

The Ingredients
It is interesting to note that there were five forms of the Burnt Offering drawn from three spheres and now there are five forms of the Meat Offering, also drawn from three spheres. The Burnt Offering, drawn from the three spheres of herd, flock or fowls, might be a bullock, a sheep, a goat, turtle doves or pigeons, five forms. The Meat Offering was of fine flour with oil and frankincense. It might be offered either as unbaked flour, or as an Offering baked in the oven (v.4), or baked on a flat plate (v.5), or in a frying pan (v.7), or indeed it could be firstfruits, green ears of corn which would be ground into flour (v.14). Again five forms from three spheres. Those who have an interest in Bible Numerals will doubtless note the recurrence of the numbers five and three throughout the story of the Offerings.

The flour, oil, frankincense, firstfruits and salt are all types of the Saviour in some way and it will be important to see too that there was to be no leaven nor any honey in the Meat Offering. The reason for the exclusion of leaven and honey will become apparent.

The Fineness of the Flour
The flour was the substantive part of the Meat Offering

and it was "fine" flour. B.W.Newton says of this, "The word thus translated means flour fully ground, finely sifted, and consequently freed from all roughness". It was the finest of fine meal. How beautifully this portrays our Lord's perfection of character. There was no harshness in Him, neither was there any one virtue that shone out greater than another. All was perfectly balanced and blended. He was full of grace and truth. He could expound truth to Nicodemus the learned Rabbi in John ch 3 and He could minister grace to a poor woman of Samaria in John ch 4, and this principle is repeated again and again throughout the four Gospels. This is why we speak of His moral glory. The choicest of men and of His disciples were at times guilty of imbalance. Some particular feature was predominant. So we speak of the patience of Job, the faith of Abraham, the meekness of Moses, the wisdom of Solomon, the courage of Daniel, the zeal of Peter, the knowledge of Paul and the love of John. One particular virtue outshone the others. These were good men. They were morally good and great but not morally glorious. Only our blessed Lord could be truly typified by fine flour.

Again, fine flour is malleable, unresisting. It will accept any form into which it is pressed and the Lord Jesus in every and any circumstance of life bowed without hesitation to the will of His Father. He could say, "I delight to do thy will, O my God; yea, thy law is within my heart" (Psalm 40. v 8). He came to do the will of God, He did it, He did it perfectly and He delighted to do it, and in the most adverse circumstances He did not fail. It is surely the endeavour of every sincere and thoughtful believer to do God's will, but are we not at times self-willed? Do we not on occasions walk in the way of our own pleasing? Only the blessed Saviour could say, "I do always those things that please Him" (John ch 8. v 29) for His every thought, word and deed, His every movement, was with the intent of bringing pleasure to His Father. How true are those words –

> *The fine flour in its beauty*
> *The perfect Man portrays,*
> *In all His path of duty,*
> *In all His heavenly ways.*
>   I.Y.Ewan

Another has written, "Fine gold is gold of the purest metal, gold undimmed by the least tarnish. Fine linen is linen of the finest thread. So fine flour is flour of the first quality, flour freed from every particle of grit or coarseness" (F. H. White)

The Fullness of the Oil

Oil was applied to the Meat Offering in several ways. Indeed three different words are used to describe these varied applications. Sometimes the flour would be "mingled" with the oil (v.5). Sometimes the baked Offering would be "anointed" with oil (v.4). Again, the oil may at times be "poured" (v.1) so that the flour would be saturated with oil. Mingled, anointed, poured. How significant do these become when we view the oil as being a symbol of the person and ministry of the Holy Spirit.

Mingled

The words of Gabriel to Mary are in perfect keeping with the symbol of the flour mingled with oil. "The Holy Ghost shall come upon thee, and the power of the Highest shall overshadow thee: therefore also that holy thing which shall be born of thee shall be called the Son of God" (Luke ch 1 v 35). Here is the mystery of our Lord's conception in the womb of the virgin! We are not asked to explain or to understand, only to believe, and wonder, that divinely, miraculously, the Holy Child was conceived in Mary's virgin womb by the power of the Spirit of God. It was as if the flour was mingled with the oil.

Anointed

It was an historical, memorable day when, at thirty years of age the Saviour stood in the River Jordan. Somewhat reluctantly the faithful John Baptist had agreed to baptize

Him, and then, "The Holy Ghost descended in bodily shape like a dove and abode upon Him" (Luke ch 3 v 22). It was but a short time after that, that He came in His ministry to Nazareth where He had been brought up. He came to the synagogue which He knew so well and He stood up indicating His desire to read the Scriptures. He calmly found the place which we now know as Isaiah 61 and read "The Spirit of the Lord is upon me, because he hath anointed me" (Luke 4.18). Those were the early days of an anointed ministry. The flour had been anointed with the oil.

To this anointed ministry Peter refers in His preaching to the nation on the Day of Pentecost, "Ye men of Israel, hear these words; Jesus of Nazareth, a man approved of God among you by miracles and wonders and signs, which God did by him in the midst of you, as ye yourselves also know" (Acts ch 2. v 22), and again, at a later date, "God anointed Jesus of Nazareth with the Holy Ghost and with power: who went about doing good, and healing all that were oppressed of the devil; for God was with Him"

Poured
It was a ministry in total fellowship with the gracious Spirit when, typically, the oil was poured upon the flour. The word "poured" is the same Hebrew word as in Psalm 45. v 2, "grace is "poured" into thy lips". The flour was saturated with the oil. There was an unbroken communion between Son and Spirit in the ministry of the Saviour.

The fruit of the Spirit (Gal ch 5. v 22; Eph ch 5. v 9) was therefore seen in all its fullness in the life and ministry of the Lord Jesus. It pervaded all that He was and all that He did. There was love, joy, peace, longsuffering, gentleness, goodness, faith, meekness and temperance. There was a perfect blending of every pleasing feature in His holy character. There was not more love than joy or more peace than gentleness or goodness. There was not more meekness than faith. What a delightful oneness, what a sacred fellowship there was between divine Persons.

The Handful

The flour with the oil applied was then brought by the offerer to the officiating priest, carried in a suitable vessel with an unspecified quantity of frankincense in the vessel also. A handful of the flour with the oil was then offered upon the altar to be burnt there as an Offering made by fire. There is some difference of opinion as to whether the offerer or the priest is referred to when we read, "he shall take thereout his handful of the flour thereof, and of the oil thereof". Perhaps the majority view is that, since the handful is now to be placed on the altar it is the priest who takes out the handful and approaches the altar. There is of course, no doubt in Leviticus ch.12 that it is the priest who there takes his handful and since all believers today are priests, it does not materially affect the typical teaching. B.W.Newton remarks, "When the Meat Offering had been thus prepared, the priest was directed to grasp all that his hand could grasp ... and to place it on the altar".

As is often pointed out, some hands would be larger, or smaller, than others. Jehovah only asks that the hand should be full, whatever its size. So it is today, that believer-priests have differing measures of appreciation and varying degrees of apprehension, knowledge and ability. All that is asked of us is that the hand should indeed be full as we bring our personal thoughts of Christ to the Father.

The Frankincense

Frankincense, (Heb *lebonah,* Strong 3828) was a fragrant perfume, white, pure, and precious. Indeed it was so called because of its whiteness, which signifies the essential purity of the Lord Jesus. It may be remembered that frankincense was mixed with other spices to produce the sweet incense which was laid up in the Tabernacle (Exod ch 30.vv 34-36). However, while a handful of the flour and oil of the Meat Offering was placed upon the altar, all the frankincense must be offered there. There is preciousness in the Son of God which God alone can fully appreciate.

> *But the high mysteries of His Name*
> *An angel's grasp transcend;*
> *The Father only, glorious claim,*
> *The Son can comprehend.*
>
> Josiah Conder

The intense fire of the altar would cause the frankincense to exude its fragrance and so all the adverse circumstances of life only but brought out the sweetness of the Saviour's character. It was so even until the last, for as men were nailing Him to the cross, His only cry was, "Father forgive them".

The Baked Offering.

It has already been briefly noted that although the Meat Offering may be of unbaked flour mingled with oil, yet at times the offerer may bring a baked Offering, and this baked Offering could be prepared in any one of three different ways, either in the oven, on a flat plate, or in a frying-pan.

The Oven.

There now arises a problem here, and a difference of opinion among expositors. It is obvious of course, and all agree, that the suffering here typified by the oven is a suffering hidden from view. Away from the eyes of men our blessed Lord indeed suffered. But when?

The thought at once comes to many that this must surely be those dark hours when as a lonely sin-bearer He endured wrath and agony that no human eye did or could behold, and that this was the Oven suffering. The problem with this interpretation is that the Meat Offering is not in any way concerned with sin-bearing. This Offering is an oblation, a gift of appreciation and gratitude. Can a gift be offered in connection with forgiveness of sins? But then it must be asked, where else did the Saviour suffer hidden from the eyes of men?

Perhaps we should think of those weeks which He spent in

the loneliness of the Judean wilderness, confronted by the Devil. He suffered there alone. No disciple observed what happened in that lonely desert experience. Anything that we now know must have been revealed by inspiration but it was surely an oven experience. For thirty years Jesus as the fine flour had been seen in Nazareth. He walked its streets, He sat in its synagogue, He worked as a carpenter. It was a perfect unblemished life lived among men for all of those years. Now He is in the desert and He is alone. This solitary Man must now endure the onslaught of Satan. He is to be tried as to His dependence upon God, as to His obedience, and as to His patience. Will the dependant Man turn stones to bread to meet His own need? No! Will He spectacularly throw Himself down from the heights to test the promise of Psalm 91. v 11? No! Will He pay homage to Satan in return for rule over the kingdoms of men? Never! These have already been promised to Him in Psalm 2. v 8 and He can, in patience, await God's time. The Devil leaves Him! How much He endured during those days in the Judean wilderness, hungry and alone with no human companion or friend! Is this not the oven-like suffering of the Son of God?

The Pan

What a contrast, for this "pan" (Hebrew *machabath*, Strong 4227) was a flat plate, completely open to view. It was similar to that which is called in some countries a "griddle", and in others a "girdle". Unleavened flour mingled with oil would be cooked on this flat plate, then parted in pieces and oil poured upon the pieces. It has been noted that there is no thought of death in the Meat Offering, but what symbols of suffering there are! The fierce heat of the oven and now the intense heat of the flat plate. Whether it is pierced cakes baked in the oven or wafers baked and pressed, there was indeed a real suggestion of suffering. But the Meat Offering baked on the flat plate had this added dimension that all was open for men to see. Had they not indeed seen the Saviour weeping? He wept with the bereaved sisters at Bethany and men saw

His tears and said, "Behold, how He loved Him". And did they not see Him wail over Jerusalem as He looked across from the Mount of Olives? (Luke ch 19. v 41). But O that awful sight at Golgotha when, hanging in agony He could cry prophetically, "All they that see me laugh me to scorn: they shoot out the lip, they shake the head ...They gaped upon me with their mouths ... they look and stare upon me" (Psalm 22. vv 7,13,17). It was suffering as on a flat plate for all to behold.

The Fryingpan

This was a pan with sides. Whereas that which was baked in the oven was completely concealed and that which was baked on the flat plate was entirely open for all to view, that which was cooked in the frying pan was partly concealed and partly open to view. May it not be said that the closer one came the more one could see and appreciate, whereas those who remained at a distance would only have a partial apprehension? Some believers indeed live very close to the Lord Jesus and have great appreciation of His sufferings. Others follow afar off and do not have that depth of appreciation which their friends have. May we all draw nearer so that we may have a deeper affection for Him who suffered so much for us. May we sing sincerely –

> Draw me nearer, nearer, nearer blessed Lord
> To thy precious wounded side.

The Priestly Portion

It has been observed that the Burnt Offering was sometimes referred to as the whole Burnt Offering since it was all, in its entirety apart from the skin, devoted to God and to the altar. Men did not eat any of the Burnt Offering. The Meat Offering was different in this respect for while there was indeed a memorial handful of it burnt on the altar, the greater portion was given to Aaron and to his sons. "That which is left of the Meat Offering shall be Aaron's and his sons': it is a thing most holy of the offerings of the LORD made by fire" (v.10).

It is a precious thought that while a handful of the Meat

Offering was burning on the altar and a sweet savour was ascending to heaven, the priestly family was feeding on that which was delightful to God. The handful was called a memorial, speaking to God by its sweet savour of the fragrant life of His Son, and men were now permitted to enjoy that very same thing. What a gracious provision is this, that we are allowed, and able, to satisfy ourselves with that which has already satisfied the Father.

The Exclusions.

It remains, before considering the firstfruits, to note those two ingredients which were forbidden, which must not be included in the Meat Offering. "No Meat Offering, which ye shall bring unto the LORD, shall be made with leaven: for ye shall burn no leaven, nor any honey, in any offering of the LORD made by fire" (v.11).

No Leaven

Leaven and honey are opposites in their actions. Leaven is a corrupting element. It will soon corrupt any flour to which it is added. For this reason it is always viewed in Scripture as a symbol of evil. The Lord Jesus used it in this way and spoke of the leaven of the Pharisees and of the Sadducees (Matt ch 16. v 6), and the leaven of Herod (Mark ch 8.v 15), and even in His parable in Matthew ch 13. v 33 the leaven which the Saviour spoke of was the leaven of evil teaching in the kingdom. Paul used it in this way too in his epistles and wrote of the leaven of malice and wickedness (1 Cor ch 5. v 8). Until this very day Jewish women will ritually sweep the house before the eating of the Passover meal, searching for any crumbs of leaven

No such symbol must be included in this Meat Offering, but it must be noted that there was in Leviticus ch 23. v 13 a new Meat Offering which was baked with leaven. What is the meaning? The Meat Offering of Leviticus ch 2 is typical of Christ personally but the new Meat Offering, the two loaves of Leviticus ch 23, offered at Pentecost, is typical of the

Church. Where men are concerned there will always be leaven but there must be no leaven in that which typifies the unblemished Christ.

No Honey

Perhaps it seems strange that there should be no honey, for is not honey a sweet substance, and is used in this way in other parts of the Word? (Psalm 19. v 10). This indeed is true but in typical Scriptures speaking of Christ honey is not suitable for it is easily fermented and may become sour. It is perhaps symbolic of a natural human sweetness, an amiability which, when the truth is applied to it, often turns sour. How many an apparently gracious believer, when confronted with, say, the truth of baptism, has lost his sweetness and may indeed become hostile. There was no such changeable sweetness in the Saviour. He remained His gracious self whatever men said or did to Him, as we have seen when He was being nailed to the cross.

To quote Newberry, "That which was burnt as incense upon the altar was subject to the testing fire of the altar. Nothing therefore, which could not stand that test might be offered there. Honey appears to represent that sweetness and amiability of disposition which might be simply natural affection; but such sweetness – precious, excellent as it is in its place – will not bear the test of divine holiness in any individual born after the flesh"

Notice the contrasts. There must be frankincense, but no honey. Both are sweet but the heat which would ferment the honey would but bring out the fragrance of the frankincense. There must be salt, but no leaven. Salt is the great preservative; leaven is that which corrupts. It is as if the Lord is, in a dual way, emphasising the sinlessness of Christ. Salt yes, but no leaven. Put into the Offering that which preserves the freshness. Exclude from the Offering that which would corrupt. God's Son is not only sinless, He is impeccable, He cannot sin. This is doubly indicated.

The Offering of Firstfruits

A casual reading of the latter part of Leviticus ch 2 might appear to reveal a kind of contradiction, but such, of course, cannot be in the divine Word. The perceived problem is that in v.12 there is reference to firstfruits which may be offered but are not to be burned on the altar. However, in v.14 there are instructions regarding fruitfruits which are indeed to be burned on the altar.

Apart from the fact that there are two different Hebrew words used for "firstfruits" the typical significance is very beautiful. The firstfruits of v.12 are the firstfruits of the harvest as in Leviticus ch 23. These typify Christ risen as the firstfruits of those who believe, the Church (1 Cor ch 15. v 20). Such a Christ, raised from the dead, will never be taken back to the altar. But the firstfruits of v.14 are green ears of corn, Christ in the prime of His perfect Manhood, on His way to the altar. Such a young Man He was, parched by the fire and bruised by suffering as we have seen. "Full ears", so He was a "Man of sorrows" but morally full and complete before God, and as such went willingly to the altar. May we daily feast more and more on such a Saviour, God's food and ours. May we, like the Father, find our satisfaction in Him.

Christ in the Peace Offering

Introductory

The Peace Offering is the third of those Offerings which are referred to as "the sweet savour" Offerings. It has earlier been observed that it holds the central place in this first account of the Offerings in the earlier chapters of Leviticus. First was the Burnt Offering, all for God. This is followed by the Meat Offering, then the Peace Offering, and these are three sweet-savour Offerings. After these comes the Sin Offering and then the Trespass Offering and there is only one fleeting reference to sweet savour in connection with the guilt Offerings, which will be noticed later (Lev ch 4.v 31). The order is very significant and instructive, for the first two Offerings bring pleasure to God and the last two bring forgiveness to men while in this central Peace Offering God and men meet and together share what they have found in Christ. It is a fellowship Offering.

When however, we come to the Law of the Offerings in later chapters the order is changed and the Peace Offering comes last of all. Two reasons have been suggested. First, peace is the ultimate in our experience. This is what God has in mind for His people and when we fully arrive here there is nothing to follow. It is the apex, the rest of God, and the eternal joy of those who have been to the altar, to the cross and sacrifice of Christ. Second, perhaps it is only when we have truly entered into the meaning of Calvary as seen in the earlier Offerings that we then arrive at the peace which God has for us. We see what Christ means to God in the Burnt Offering and the Meat Offering. We learn what Christ is for us in the Offerings for our sin and our trespasses, and in the full realization of all this we are at peace.

The Purpose of the Peace Offering

The questions might be asked, "Why did a man bring a Peace Offering? On what occasions was it more suitable than other Offerings?"

Picture three men on their way to the altar, each bringing a Peace Offering. We ask the first, "Why a Peace Offering?" He will tell us that it is for thanksgiving (Lev ch 7. vv 12,15). He has been granted some particular favour of the Lord, maybe some answer to his prayers and he wants to render thanks to the Lord for his peace and prosperity so he will offer a Peace Offering as in the Scriptures just quoted.

The same question is addressed to the second man. Is his Offering for thanksgiving? He will tell us "No". This man is making a vow, a solemn promise to God concerning some matter, and he wants to solemnize his vow at the altar with an Offering. So he will offer a Peace Offering in accordance with Leviticus ch 7. v 16.

The third man is asked the same but his Offering is neither for any special thanksgiving nor for a vow. His is just a voluntary Offering as in Leviticus ch 7. v 16. There is no particular reason for his Offering as there was with the first two men. He just wants to give something to God out of a full heart and a Peace Offering seems to be the most suitable and acceptable way of doing this.

But, we might say to these three men, "Why a Peace Offering, why not a Burnt Offering?" They will then tell us that this is a fellowship Offering. They want to give to God that which the Priestly family and their own families and friends can all share with them. This would not be possible with a Burnt Offering, which, as we have seen, was all for God and the altar. This fellowshipping in the Peace Offering will be considered later.

So then, whether for thanksgiving, or for a vow, or purely a voluntary Offering, all are solemnized at the altar. For the believer today this is Calvary. At the cross all our spiritual exercises are acceptable to, and accepted by, the Lord. We render thanks, we make our vows, and we worship, in the shadow of Golgotha.

It must be pointed out that in no instance did the offerer bring his Peace Offering for forgiveness of sins, or to obtain peace or make peace. For whichever of the three reasons mentioned the offerer brought his Offering he did so in a conscious enjoyment of peace. In peace of mind and heart he was in a condition to truly give thanks, to make his vows, or to worship.

The Plurality!

It is important to notice that "Peace" here is a plural word, in Hebrew *shelemim,* plural of the noun *shelem* (Strong 8002) but the plurality is lost in translation and is in fact almost untranslatable. It would not make for intelligible reading in English to say "Peaces Offering" or "Sacrifice of Peaces" yet this is, literally, what is said in Hebrew. The reason is that at times the Hebrew used the plural, not to signify a plurality as we understand it, in contrast to the singular, but to indicate completeness, fullness, magnificence, plenitude. So it is used here. An example of such a plural is found in Isaiah ch 53. v 9 where the Saviour is said to be "with the rich in His death". "Death" here is a plural, "deaths". Of course our Lord died but once, but such was the greatness of that death and of all that was accomplished in it that nothing more could have been accomplished had He died a thousand deaths. His once-for-all death at Calvary was all sufficient, majestic, wondrous, and in Hebrew this is signified by the use of the plural.

It will be remembered that on His last evening, just before He left His disciples, Jesus said to them, "Peace I leave with you, my peace I give unto you" (John ch 14. v 27). Is there a plural implied here? And does not Paul convey a similar thought when he writes, "Now the Lord of peace Himself give you peace always by all means"? (2 Thess ch 3. v 16).

Male or Female

In certain respects the Peace Offering was similar to the Burnt Offering, being either from the herd or from the flock, and always without blemish, but now there is a notable difference in that the Peace Offering may be either male or female whereas the Burnt Offering was of males only, sons of the herd. The characteristics of both male and female may be seen in Him who is our Peace Offering. He has the power, the strength and initiative which is expected of the male, but perfectly blended with this He has that gentleness, that beautiful submissiveness and tenderness of the female. In such perfection of character He walked resolutely to Calvary and offered Himself there unresisting and without complaint.

The Presentation

As it was with other offerings (Lev ch 1 v.4; ch 4. v 4) the offerer must now present his Offering at the door of the Tabernacle and lean his hand upon its head signifying his personal identification with the Offering, as if to say, "This is mine, my Offering". He himself must then kill it, and as has been remarked in the notes on the Burnt Offering in this commentary, it is rather ironic that the offerer is responsible for the very death which is to bring him blessing. It is in the grace and goodness of God that though our sins have occasioned the death of His Son yet in that death is the forgiveness of those very sins, and many blessings beside.

The Fellowship Offering

The Peace Offering is truly a fellowship Offering, for, as has already been noted, God and the priests, the offerer and his family and friends will all feast upon the one and same sacrifice. But God must have His portion first, to be burned on the altar. Jehovah must have the fat that covered the inwards, the two kidneys and the fat upon them and the caul over the liver. Notice that the word "fat" in the Peace Offering is different to that used for the fat of the Burnt Offering. With this latter it was the fat on the limbs, associated with what another has called "manifested devotedness – devotedness exhibited in action. Accordingly, the limbs of the animal, which typify powers of developed action, and the outer fat belonging to those limbs, were there made the prominent parts of the Offering" (B.W.Newton). The limbs and their fat were, in the Burnt Offering, burned on the altar for God. The fat of the Peace Offering however, was the fat associated with the inwards, which might be termed the suet, and the limbs were not burned at all. The priests would then take the blood and sprinkle or strew it round about the altar, evidence of the death and acceptability of the Offering. Although this was not a Sin Offering still, in all our approach to God we are reminded that such is not possible apart from the shedding of blood.

The various parts of the animal to be burned on the altar are now detailed as follows. "the fat that covereth the inwards, and all the fat that is upon the inwards, And the two kidneys, and the fat that is on them, which is by the flanks, and the caul above the liver, with the kidneys, it shall he take away" vv.8,9. Keil & Delitzsch comment that the portions mentioned comprehended all the separable fat in the inside of the sacrificial animal. Hence they were also designated "all the fat" of the sacrifice. C.H.M. remarks that "The most excellent portion of the sacrifice was laid on God's altar. The inward parts, the hidden energies, the tender sensibilities of the blessed Jesus, were devoted to God as the only One who could perfectly enjoy them"

The fat is a symbol of the richness and excellence of the Offering and a reminder of the inner excellence of the Lord Jesus. Newberry notes that the parts here specified, especially the kidneys, were those in which the inward fat chiefly abounds. He adds, "Where there is vigour in the powers of inward being, and where that inward vigour is found meet for the altar, there, there must indeed be perfectness. But where was such perfectness found? Only in Him who gave Himself for us, an Offering and sacrifice to God for a sweet-smelling savour"

The kidneys are used frequently as indicating the innermost seat of man's desires and affections. Often in the K.J.V. the word is translated "reins" as in, "God trieth the hearts and *reins*" (Psalm 7. v 9). "Examine me O LORD, and prove me; try my *reins* and my heart" (Psalm 26. v 2). "O LORD of hosts, that judgest righteously, that triest the *reins* and the heart" (Jer ch

11. v 20). "I the LORD search the heart, I try the *reins*" Jer ch 17. v 10).

The "caul above the liver" has occasioned some difficulty among commentators but a consensus of opinion seems to indicate that this is a protective net or membrane which covered the kidneys, the spleen, and other internal organs.

In connection with the Offering of a sheep, the instructions are much the same as for the bullock or goat, but with this addition. The "whole rump" of the sheep is mentioned in Leviticus ch 3. v 9. This is, literally, the "fat tail". Oriental sheep had an especially heavy tail, sometimes weighing as much as 15lbs. or more. It was a rich mixture of marrow and fat and in its entirety it was to be burned on the altar fire along with the parts already referred to.

So, all these parts of the Peace Offering constituted God's portion, and all rose in a sweet savour to Him, a foregleam of Him who was to come, Prince of Peace who would satisfy the desires of the heart of God and be a delight to believing men too, men who would learn to sing, "Now none but Christ can satisfy".

The Portion of Priests and People
As has already been mentioned, this was a fellowship Offering in which God, the priests, the Offerer, and their respective families would all share. While God's portion burned upon the altar the officiating priest would carry away the breast and the right shoulder. These were termed "the wave breast" and "the heave shoulder" and would be the food of the priestly family. The breast, which was for the priestly family in general, would be elevated and waved to and fro for the eye of God to behold. The right shoulder was the portion of the officiating priest. It would be lifted up similarly but probably because of its weight it would be simply raised before God.

The shoulder is of course, an obvious symbol of strength and power, and the breast a symbol of love and affection. These features of His Son are delightful to God and it is a matter for profound thanksgiving that we who are a priestly family are permitted to eat of that which is the food of the altar, satisfying God.

When God and the priests have had their portion then there was much of the Offering yet left. This the offerer would now carry home. Perhaps he would prepare a feast, and around his table sharing with him would be his own family and maybe his friends and neighbours. Well do believers sing, "What a fellowship, what a joy divine". God, priests, and people all enjoying the same food and all the while a sweet savour ascending from the altar fire to God.

Prohibitions in the Offering
It has been observed that there were three reasons why a man might bring a Peace Offering. It might be a thanksgiving, or in connection with the making of a vow, or perhaps just a voluntary Offering out of a full heart, but there were regulations or restrictions associated with every Peace Offering whatever the reason for it might be

The Peace Offering for Thanksgiving.
In the case of an Offering for thanksgiving that portion of the Offering which would be eaten must be eaten the same day that it was offered, none of it must remain until the morning. Thanksgiving does not require a great deal of spirituality, it is almost an expected courtesy that a man should give thanks for that which has been given to him. If then there is a lack of any deep spirituality there may well be an associated carelessness and the duty to give thanks could be forgotten. Thanksgiving should therefore be offered the same day, the day in which the Offering was presented at the altar, when the exercise was still fresh in the offerer's mind. It must not be left until the morning for a night of sleep may result in forgetfulness and so the necessary thankfulness may be forgotten.

There may also be the possibility that if it is not all eaten on that day some may think that the offerer is reserving something of the Offering for his own private use, whereas, having been devoted to Jehovah, the flesh of the Offering must now be shared with friends and ideally it could be used to feast the poor.

Notice with this Offering there are unleavened cakes and wafers anointed with oil, but also leavened bread (Lev ch 7. v 12). It is a reminder that in our holiest moments there is a remembrance that by nature we are sinners and it is only of the grace of God that we are permitted to draw near to Him and commune with Him and with others.

The Peace Offering and the Vow

In this case those who eat of the Offering may do so on the day that it was offered, but also on the next day. Might this be a recognition of rather more spirituality in an offerer who will readily enter into a vow before the Lord? Such a man will not easily forget his intentions, even on the next day. But after that, on the third day, it must not be eaten. Indeed not only would it not be accepted nor imputed to the offerer but it would be an abomination and those who did eat of it must bear the consequences of their disobedience. For the believer today the lesson is that it is necessary to stay near to the altar, to Calvary. If we stray too far from the cross our exercises can become mechanical and unacceptable to God.

Practically too, in those warm regions of the world it is difficult to keep flesh in its purity after the second day. So, in a defiling world, our exercises may go stale or even sour, and unacceptable, if there is delay in our presentation to God of that which we have enjoyed of spiritual things.

The Peace Offering in Worship.

The directions for this Peace Offering are similar to those which pertained to that which is offered with a vow, just considered. It may be eaten on the day of the Offering and also on the second day, but not at all after that. Especially must we remember to stay close to the cross and in the shades of Calvary so that we shall be better conditioned to enjoy communion with God and with one another, and worship.

No Uncleanness

In three verses in chapter 7 (19-21) it is emphasised that there must be no uncleanness of any kind associated with the Peace Offering. Otherwise the consequences are solemn indeed. "All that be clean shall eat thereof. But the soul that eateth of the flesh of the sacrifice of peace offerings, that pertain unto the LORD, having his uncleanness upon him, even that soul shall be cut off from his people. Moreover the soul that shall touch any unclean thing, as the uncleanness of man, or any unclean beast, or any abominable unclean thing, and eat of the flesh of the sacrifice of peace offerings, which pertain unto the LORD, even that soul shall be cut off from his people". So highly does the Lord esteem holiness in His people that ignoring His prohibitions will result in the rejection of that person.

The parallel for believers today may be seen in 1 Corinthians where carnality had resulted in sin and marred the communion at the Lord's Supper. There was division and drunkenness, immorality and false doctrine, and God moved in governmental judgment in sickness and death. "Wherefore whosoever shall eat this bread, and drink this cup of the Lord, unworthily, shall be guilty of the body and blood of the Lord. But let a man examine himself, and so let him eat of that bread, and drink of that cup. For he that eateth and drinketh unworthily, eateth and drinketh damnation (*judgment*) to himself, not discerning the Lord's body. For this cause many are weak and sickly among you, and many sleep" (1 Cor ch 11. vv 27-30). The great preventative was, as quoted, "Let a man examine himself, and so let him eat".

His Own Hands

It was required of the offerer that he must bring his offering with his own hands. "His own hands shall bring the offerings of the LORD made by fire" (Lev ch 7. v 30). His offering must be seen to be both personal and voluntary and he himself must present his offering to the priest. Although the Lord's Supper is undoubtedly the finest example of a company enjoying the Peace Offering collectively, yet there is something very personal even about our participation there. It is imperative that each believer, both brethren and sisters alike, should come to the Supper with hearts prepared. Sisters will come to engage in silent worship and this brings an atmosphere of worship into the whole assembly. Brethren will come in the same condition of mind and heart and if there is a suitable occasion they will lead the company in expressions of gratitude to God in remembrance of His Son, and together all will, as it were, eat the Peace Offering, communing with each other and with the Father concerning Christ. Such holy fellowship is very precious to God and rises in sweet savour to Him for His pleasure. The unity expressed is good and pleasant, fragrant as the holy anointing oil which was poured upon Israel's High Priest and precious as the dew of Hermon which nourished the hills of Zion (Psalm 133). May we know more of the blessings of the Peace Offering, both individually and collectively.

Christ in the Sin Offering

Sin and Trespass

As has been mentioned earlier, some commentators, because of the close similarity between the Sin Offering and the Trespass Offering, prefer to treat these together and refer to them as the Guilt Offerings. There does however, appear to be differences which require that we must distinguish one from the other. This is very evident in the Laws of the Offerings in Leviticus ch 6 and ch7. In Chapter 6. v 25 we read "This is the Law of the Sin Offering" (Heb.*chata'ah* Strong 2403), but when we come to Chapter 7. v 1 we read "This is the Law of the Trespass Offering" (Heb.*asham* Strong 817). The differing words do seem to indicate that the two Offerings should be treated separately, and this we will seek to do in this Commentary. If at times these expressions seem to be used interchangeably then it will be remembered that sin is sin and trespass is sin and often what applies to one is equally applicable to the other and it is difficult to be explicit.

Perhaps it is important to notice that these two Offerings are essentially for the sins of a redeemed people. While there are principles which apply to men and sins in general, whether the men are saved or not, yet it must be remembered that those whose sins have been judicially dealt with and expiated by the blood of the Lamb, nevertheless do sin and the teaching of the Guilt Offerings is that all sins, by whomsoever they are committed, are grievous in the sight of God and require forgiveness in His prescribed way. For the believer in the Lord Jesus confession and forgiveness are necessary prerequisites for acceptable worship, and service.

The Sin Offering

The prevalence of the expression "if a soul shall sin through ignorance" in Leviticus ch 4, suggests that the main feature of the Sin Offering in this chapter is sin in the nature. If a man can sin and not even be aware that he has sinned, this shows that there is sin, and sinful tendencies, in his nature. Of course sins of ignorance are sins nevertheless and when they come to light they must be judged. They require an Offering and forgiveness. Leviticus ch 4 and the verses immediately following give details of these Offerings showing that the Offering is always commensurate with the individual responsibility of the person who has sinned. A Priest may sin (v.3); the whole Congregation may sin (v.13); a Ruler may sin (v.22); one of the common people may sin (v.27), and there are directions regarding the specific Offering required by each of these.

Notice how God is robbed by these sins. He is robbed of worship when a priest sins, of testimony when the congregation sins, of government when a ruler sins, and of fellowship when one of the common people sins.

THE SIN OFFERING FOR THE PRIEST (Lev ch 4. vv 3-12)

The majority of expositors seem satisfied that the anointed Priest who has sinned here is the High Priest himself, who was, in a special way "the anointed". Leviticus ch 21. v 10 is quoted in support of this. The sin of a High Priest was solemn indeed for he was the people's example and if he sinned then it may well have the effect of causing the common people to sin. The JFB Commentary writes, "that is, the high priest, in whom, considering his character as typical mediator, and his exalted office, the people had the deepest interest; and whose transgression of any part of the divine law, therefore, whether done unconsciously or heedlessly, was a very serious offence, both as regarding himself individually, and the influence of his example. He is the person principally meant, though the common order of the priesthood was included" B.W.Newton's comments are similar, "The High Priests, and all other priests, were anointed (see Lev ch 8), consequently this appellation might belong to any of them. If a priest sinned, not only would that sin incapacitate him for acting on behalf of others, but it would necessarily involve those for whom he acted. He who sins whilst representing others, or whilst teaching and guiding others, does thereby involve them also in guilt ... Hence the necessity of our having a High Priest, holy, harmless, undefiled – One who never did, and never could sin".

A Young Bullock without Blemish

Sin in any sense and in any circumstance is heinous, but the sin of a priest was especially serious and the directions and details which follow are in keeping with this. The sinning priest must bring a young bullock without blemish. Another man of lesser standing in the congregation might bring a kid of the goats (v.23), or, in the case of one of the common people, a kid of the goats or a lamb, and either of these, a female (v.28).

As it was with the Burnt Offering and the Peace Offering the offerer must bring his Offering to the door of the tabernacle and here he would lay his hand upon the bullock's head before killing it. The significance of the hand upon the head is, however, a little different with the Sin Offering. True, just as in the Burnt Offering, it signifies identification with the Offering, as if to say, "This is mine, my Offering". But whereas in the Burnt Offering all the acceptability of the Offering was being transferred to the offerer, now, in the Sin Offering, all the guilt of the sinner was being transferred to his substitute and the substitute would bear the judgment due to the sin. As another has written, "In the case of the sin-offering, there was the same principle of identity with the victim by laying on of hands; but he who came, came not as a worshipper, but as a sinner; not as clean for communion with the Lord, but as having guilt upon him; and instead of his being identified with the acceptability of the victim ... the victim became identified with his guilt and unacceptableness, bore his sins and was treated accordingly" (JND). So has all our guilt been borne by the Lord Jesus, our sinless Substitute, and our identification with Him means that the judgment due to us has been meted out to Him and we are free. "He was wounded for our transgressions, He was bruised for our iniquities ... the Lord hath laid on Him the iniquity of us all".

The offerer himself must now kill the bullock and as has been noted earlier, he thereby finds that he is responsible for the blood-shedding and death which has purchased his forgiveness. So do we recognise that we are accountable for the death of the Saviour, God's Son. Grace alone could provide such a plan of salvation for those who believe. The children sing it often. O that they would early enter into it and that we might all rejoice in the truth of it –

> Wounded for me, wounded for me,
> There on the cross He was wounded for me.
> Gone my transgressions and now I am free,
> All because Jesus was wounded for me.

The Shed Blood
The officiating priest must now bring of the bullock's blood into the tabernacle. The atoning blood must go where the sin has gone, right into the Holy Place. To quote Newton again, "The sin of a Priest would, of course, reach those places and instruments of service which pertained to him as a Priest. It pertained to the Priest's office to stand before the Lord in the Holy Place, and to minister at the golden altar there. But a defiled foot would taint the ground on which it stood, and a defiled hand would taint the altar which it touched ... Hence the peculiar heinousness of a Priest's sin. It penetrated the sanctuary". But then he speaks of the blessed truth that, "Howsoever far the sin may have penetrated, and whatsoever it may have affected, the power of the atoning blood has followed, as it were, the sin, and penetrated where *it* had penetrated".

So, having dipped his finger in the blood, now "the priest

shall sprinkle of the blood seven times before the LORD, before the veil of the sanctuary". The beautiful veil hid the splendour of the Holiest of All from human view and directly before the veil the blood was sprinkled seven times, complete evidence and assurance that the victim's blood had been shed. Holiness was vindicated. Jehovah was honoured and propitiated. Justice was satisfied.

Some of the blood was now put upon the horns of the golden altar, here so fittingly called "the altar of sweet incense". Mingling now with the fragrance of incense was the preciousness of shed blood, and ministry at the golden altar could be resumed. The blood that remained was now poured out at the bottom of the other altar, the altar of Burnt Offering, and the taint of sin was now expunged.

The Fat and the Inwards
There is now a striking similarity with the Peace Offering regarding the fat and the inwards. In Leviticus ch 3 vv .8-10 we read of the Peace Offering, "And he shall take off from it all the fat of the bullock for the sin offering; the fat that covereth the inwards, and all the fat that is upon the inwards and the two kidneys, and the fat that is upon them, which is by the flanks, and the caul above the liver, with the kidneys, it shall he take away as it was taken off from the bullock of the sacrifice of Peace Offerings: and the priest shall burn them upon the altar of the Burnt Offering". These same parts must now be taken from off the Sin Offering and burned on the altar. While there is no specific mention here of a sweet savour, nevertheless the ascending smoke must have been appreciated by Jehovah, prefiguring as it did, the precious fragrance of the coming Man of Calvary.

It has been noted in connection with the preceding Offerings that the fat represented the very best of the Offering and the fat that covered the inwards was the richness of the inner parts. In our Lord Jesus Christ, the great Antitype, this represents what is often called "His inner excellence". There was that in Him which could not be seen by man but which was precious to God. His thoughts and feelings, His affections, desires, and motives all brought pleasure to His Father and God, who alone could fully appreciate.

In a solemn concluding ceremony the remains of the bullock were to be burned outside the camp. "And the skin of the bullock, and all his flesh, with his head, and with his legs, and his inwards, and his dung, even the whole bullock shall he carry forth without the camp unto a clean place, where the ashes are poured out, and burn him on the wood with fire: where the ashes are poured out shall he be burnt". This was the place of judgment. See the comment on verses 11 and 12 later.

THE SIN OFFERING FOR THE CONGREGATION (Lev 4.13-21)
It is not definitively clear how the whole congregation of Israel could have sinned in ignorance, but one has only to look around today to observe how many congregations of believers are indeed sinning in ignorance. How many plain truths of the Word of God are either unknown or unheeded, such as the truth and practice of believers' Baptism, and how many unscriptural practices, such as clerisy and the ordination of clerics, are freely accepted without question? So many believers too, are apparently not aware of the sin of sectarianism, and continue, often in sincerity, if in ignorance, to gather to divisive names rather than to the Name of the Lord Jesus alone.

The responsible elders in the congregation must, on behalf of the congregation, acknowledge and confess the sin, and bring a young bullock to the tabernacle. Having laid their hands on the head of the Offering either the same elders or a representative priest would kill it before the Lord. Some of the blood must then be brought into the tabernacle to be sprinkled seven times before the veil, and the remainder of the blood must then be poured out at the bottom or foundation of the altar of Burnt Offering. Atoning blood lies at the very foundation of everything connected with the altar. Calvary is the foundation and basis of all our service, worship, and communion.

There is now a correspondence between the Offering for the congregation and the Offering for the Priest in that all the fat of the bullock as detailed in the Priest's Offering, also known as "the first bullock" (Lev ch 4. v 21) must be burned on the altar to ascend in smoke to Jehovah. As for the carcass of the bullock it must now be carried outside the camp and burned to ashes.

It seems an appropriate place to mention again that there are two Hebrew words for "burn", and both words are used in close proximity in this chapter.

In verses 10 and 19 the word is the Hebrew *qatar* (Strong 6999) which means "to burn as incense; to turn into fragrance by fire". So was the fat, with the hidden inwards, burned on the altar to rise in fragrant smoke to God.

In verses 12 and 21 the word is the Hebrew *seraph* (Strong 8313).which means "to burn utterly" So was the bullock consumed in judgment fire without the camp.

Without the Camp
"Without the camp" was a most solemn and serious place. Adam Clarke, commenting on the expression in connection with the sinning Priest in verses 11 and 12, writes, "This was intended figuratively to express the sinfulness of this sin, and the availableness of the atonement. The sacrifice, as having the sin of the priest transferred from himself to it by his confession and imposition of hands, had become unclean and abominable, and was carried, as it were, out of the Lord's sight; from the tabernacle and congregation it must be carried without the camp, and thus its own offensiveness was removed, and the sin of the person on whose behalf it was offered ... Hebrews ch 13 vv 11-13 applies this in the most pointed manner to Christ: 'For the bodies of those beasts whose blood is brought into the sanctuary by the high priest

for sin, are burned without the camp. Wherefore Jesus also, that he might sanctify the people with his own blood, suffered without the gate. Let us go forth therefore unto him without the camp, bearing his reproach'"

Another has written very helpfully, "Outside the camp was the place of the defiled (Num ch 5. v 2) and the place of the condemned (Num ch 15. vv 35-36); the place of the execution of those on whom judgment without mercy was pronounced" (J.R.Caldwell). The whole bullock was carried without the camp and was there utterly consumed in judgment fire.

The Ashes
The ashes of the Sin Offering, like those of the Burnt Offering, were most important typically, for the ashes were the memorial and the evidence that the sacrifice had been offered and the fire had burned itself out. B.W.Newton comments that "It is worthy of note that the Hebrew name for the ashes of the altar, and for "fatness" is the same, because much of the fatness and excellency of that which had been burned on the altar was in those ashes". So we read that the priest must "carry forth the ashes without the camp unto a clean place" (Lev ch 6.v 11). How beautifully typical was this of the taking down of the body of the Lord Jesus from the cross and His burial in the tomb of Joseph of Arimathaea. This was a tomb in which never man before had lain. It was undefiled by death. It was "a clean place", and so closely associated with Calvary the altar, that John records, "Now in the place where He was crucified there was a garden, and in the garden a sepulchre, wherein was never man yet laid. There laid they Jesus therefore ...for the sepulchre was nigh at hand" (John ch 19. vv 41-42). Having suffered outside the city, outside the camp, in judgment for the sins of others His sacred body was gently and reverently buried in a clean place.

THE SIN OFFERING FOR THE RULER (Leviticus ch 4. vv 22-27; ch 6. vv 24-30)
There have always been those men who have been ordained

of the Lord to guide and direct His people, to assume responsibility and care for them. The word "ruler" (Heb *nasiy* Strong 5387) indicated any person of high political standing among the people. It was used of princes, judges, and at times of kings. It was a sad and serious matter when such fell into sin, even though ignorantly, or unintentionally. Though it may be a sin of ignorance the man is guilty nevertheless and must come with confession and an Offering. Even under Law God was gracious and the sinner could be forgiven, but only on the grounds of blood shed. Today we rejoice in the reality of that of which the Offerings were but a shadow. The Son of God has come, and "what the law could not do, in that it was weak through the flesh, God sending his own Son in the likeness of sinful flesh, and for sin, condemned sin in the flesh" (Rom ch 8.vv 3-4).

A Kid of the Goats

Since the rulers did not function in the sanctuary or in holy things, as the priests did, their sin may have seemed in a sense, somewhat less serious than the sin of a priest, although all sin was heinous to God. So, whereas the sinning Priest was required to bring a bullock, the sinning ruler was to bring a kid of the goats, a male without blemish. As with other Offerings the ruler would then lay his hand upon the head of the goat and kill it. His guilt was transferred to a substitute. Another life would be sacrificed for his sin. So, for those who believe, "Christ died for our sins" (1 Cor ch 15 v .3). Another has died in our place.

> *His the curse, the wounds, the gall*
> *His the stripes - He bore them all.*
> *His the dying cry of pain*
> *When our sins He did sustain.*
>
> John Cennock

The Blood of the Goat

The blood of the Sin Offering for the ruler was not brought into the holy place. It was not put on the golden altar nor sprinkled before the veil, for the ruler did not minister in the holy place as did the priest. It was however, put on the horns of the altar of Burnt Offering, the brazen altar, and then poured out at the base or foundation of that altar, for this was indeed the foundation of all forgiveness and restoration. How important to note that the fat, the hidden richness of the Offering, was burned on the altar. For God it was fragrance. For man it was forgiveness. Both God and men are satisfied at the altar. Calvary is the sacred meeting place of God and men.

Eating the Sin Offering

Priestly men would then eat of the flesh of the Sin Offering. This was so only if the blood had not been carried into the sanctuary, and so it applied to the Sin Offering for the ruler (Lev ch 6. vv 26-30). "The priest that offereth it for sin shall eat it: in the holy place shall it be eaten, in the court of the tabernacle of the congregation. Whatsoever shall touch the flesh thereof shall be holy: and when there is sprinkled of the blood thereof upon any garment, thou shalt wash that whereon it was sprinkled in the holy place. But the earthen vessel wherein it is sodden shall be broken: and if it be sodden in a brasen pot, it shall be both scoured, and rinsed in water. All the males among the priests shall eat thereof: it is most holy. And no sin offering, whereof any of the blood is brought into the tabernacle of the congregation to reconcile withal in the holy place, shall be eaten: it shall be burnt in the fire". It must be eaten in the court, in the holy place. By this eating of the Offering the priests were, in symbol, digesting the awful reality of the sin, and grieving for it in holiness. It was their responsibility as priests to care for the people, mourning when there was sin and rejoicing when there was forgiveness. Note that the Sin Offering was most holy. So it was with our Saviour. Even when laden with our sins as our Substitute He was personally and intrinsically holy. How this holiness of the Sin Offering is emphasised in these verses. Even the very pots which were used in its preparation were to be cleansed. If they were brazen vessels they must be scoured and rinsed in water, and if they were earthenware they must be broken. The essential, intrinsic holiness of Christ must be guarded, even in the types.

THE SIN OFFERING FOR THE COMMON PEOPLE (Leviticus ch 4. vv 27-35)

There is something peculiarly precious to God in the forgiveness and restoration of one of the common people. Many will remember that during our Lord's ministry it was "the common people" who "heard Him gladly" (Mark ch 12. v 37). When the richer, more learned, sophisticated people, often refused His ministry, the common people received it. The great majority of the populace of Israel was composed of "the common people" even in Moses' day and Jehovah graciously made special provision for them when they sinned.

A Kid of the Goats

The Offering prescribed for one of the common people was similar to the Sin Offering for the ruler except that the goat was to be a female whereas that for the ruler was to be a male. The male indicates activity, initiative, and responsibility whereas the female suggests a more passive character. Perhaps, although the ruler had sinned in ignorance, there is the thought that maybe, in his position, he should have known better while the commoner would have had less opportunity to know and may indeed have been led astray by others.

Having presented his Offering the man must now, as in other cases, lay his hand upon its head in identification and then slay it in the very place where Burnt Offerings were killed, on the north side of the altar. The priest would now take of the blood and put it on the horns of the brazen altar. All that remained of the blood must be poured out at the bottom of that same altar.

The Sweet Savour!

The priest would now take away all the fat exactly as he did in the case of the Peace Offering, and burn it on the altar for a sweet savour (v.31). It is interesting that this is the one and only reference to sweet savour in the story of the Guilt Offerings. How precious, it must be said again, how precious must the forgiveness of one of the common people have been to God? With one of the common people He could have enjoyed sweet fellowship until sin marred that and broke the communion. Now there is atonement and forgiveness and that produces a sweet savour indeed.

If this man brought a lamb for his Sin Offering then we have a picture of Him who is the Lamb of God, meek and lowly, who was "led as a Lamb to the slaughter". He was unblemished in Himself, sinless and pure, both able and willing to bear the sins of others, and this He did at dark Calvary.

It must be noticed again that although all sin was grievous to God and must be dealt with, yet God graciously allowed for the possibility of poverty in the case of the common people. There were those who could not offer a goat or a lamb, and in such cases Jehovah would accept two turtle doves or two young pigeons. One of these would be offered as a Burnt Offering for God's pleasure and the other would be offered as a Sin Offering to meet the need of the sinner.

WILFULLY or IGNORANTLY? (Lev 5.1-13)

That this section is somewhat difficult of interpretation is admitted by most expositors. The sins which are here enumerated are in a great sense deliberate or wilful and yet with some there may be a measure of ignorance. To quote B.W.Newton again, "The sins of the fifth chapter are ... indeed, done in ignorance; but so much of voluntariness mingles with the ignorance, that they verge towards the wilful sins of the sixth chapter, and so stand contrasted with sins of ignorance properly so called, of which the fourth chapter treats. Such sins therefore, have a mediate character. They are committed in too much ignorance to be classed with the wilful sins of the sixth chapter; whilst on the other hand, there is too much of voluntariness in that ignorance to admit of their being classed with such sins of ignorance as are treated of in the fourth chapter". The sins of the fourth chapter are clearly sins of ignorance and are met by the Sin Offering, and the sins of the sixth chapter are equally clearly wilful and are met by the Trespass Offering. This does seem to signify the rather unusual nature of the sins of chapter 5.1-13, and the passage is immediately followed by the expression "And the LORD spake unto Moses, saying" which usually, if not invariably, indicates the commencement of a new subject or theme. Several offences are detailed in the section mentioned.

The Voice of Swearing (v.1)
This envisages the case of a man, a witness in court, who is adjured to give evidence, to tell what he knows. As in today's courts he is responsible to tell, on oath, the truth, the whole truth, and nothing but the truth. There is great difference of opinion as to whether the offence in question is his own or another's but for some reason he declines to give the required evidence. If it is the offence of another man, then he himself has not committed sin, but nevertheless he is guilty by not telling what he knows, whatever his reason for that may be.

Touching the unclean (vv. 2, 3)
Here is guilt by association. A man heedlessly or carelessly touches that which is ceremonially unclean. Perhaps he stumbles on the carcase of a dead animal and he himself is thereby unclean. How wise is that exhortation of the Psalmist, "Blessed is the man that walketh not in the counsel of the ungodly, nor standeth in the way of sinners, nor sitteth in the seat of the scornful". It is good not to walk, nor stand, nor sit, with the ungodly, lest we inadvertently are led into uncleanness. Poor Peter walked with them; he stood with them; and he sat with them at their fire, with disastrous consequences. (Luke ch 22. vv 54 – 55).

The Rash Oath (v.4)
A man makes a vow. He swears to do something, it may be

good or it may be bad, but his vow is made rashly with no consideration of all that will be involved. When everything comes to his knowledge he now finds that he cannot keep his vow. He cannot do what he promised to do. He is guilty. Why? He may have sincerely intended to keep his vow, but he cannot. That is not like God, who always keeps His promises and fulfils His word. Therefore the man who fails in this respect is not like God. He is ungodly. He is guilty. Ignorant of all that would be entailed he made his vow too rashly.

CONFESSION and OFFERING (vv. 5-13)

Whether wilfully or in ignorance, sin is sin, and must be judged, and because of the nature of these offences a man must bring a Trespass Offering which will be accepted as a Sin Offering. But there are regulations to be observed. He must make a full confession. This must be specific in relation to that particular sin. It is not sufficient to say, in a general way, "I have sinned and am sorry". As verse 5 says, "And it shall be, when he shall be guilty in one of these things, that he shall confess that he hath sinned in that thing". He must make a definite confession of the offence for which he is asking forgiveness.

The required Trespass Offering, which would be accepted as a Sin Offering, was to be a female from the flock, either a lamb or a kid of the goats. The priest would then make atonement for him in the manner of the Sin Offerings as described in chapter 4.

However, as we have before seen, some of the people would not be in a position to bring a lamb or a kid of the goats and in grace Jehovah would accept two turtle doves or two young pigeons. One bird would be a Sin Offering, atoning for the sin in question, and the second bird would be a Burnt Offering. So, the sinner's need would be met and God would have His portion too. The directions for the priest are expressed simply and clearly in verses 8-10. "And he shall bring them unto the priest, who shall offer that which is for the sin offering first, and wring off his head from his neck, but shall not divide it asunder. And he shall sprinkle of the blood of the sin offering upon the side of the altar; and the rest of the blood shall be wrung out at the bottom of the altar: it is a sin offering. And he shall offer the second for a burnt offering, according to the manner: and the priest shall make an atonement for him for his sin which he hath sinned, and it shall be forgiven him".

But then again, there may be one who could not even rise to bring two birds, and in this case he may bring the tenth part of an ephah of fine flour. The priest would take a memorial handful of this and burn it on the altar. He must not put either oil or frankincense on the flour for it is a Sin Offering, not a Meat Offering. An Offering without blood? How graciously Jehovah stooped to accomodate the poor of His people, and does He not do so yet? Are there not those today who by reason of age, feebleness of mind, low mental ability, or other retarding condition are unable to rise to the theological knowledge of others more privileged? Will God reject the little one who can only bring his lisping of "Gentle Jesus, meek and mild, look upon a little child"? How beautifully Thomas Newberry comments on this, writing, "In such cases divine grace condescends to human infirmity". Many may not be able to define the difference between atonement, redemption, propitiation, or substitution, but the handful of fine flour would soon be saturated in blood upon the altar and Jehovah sees and knows this. It is His appreciation of Christ which is the ground of our salvation. Still He says today, as He did to others so long ago, "When I see the blood I will pass over you" (Exodus ch 12. v 13). As B.W.Newton remarks, "Yet may not our estimate of Christ as the Sin Offering fall practically to this low standard? ...Happy for us that our interest in the Great Sacrifice depends on the fact of having believed, and not on the clearness, or comprehensiveness, or vigour of our faith!"

Note, "He shall offer that which is for the Sin Offering first".

Sin must be confessed and forgiven before the man can worship acceptably. Only when the Sin Offering has been offered and atonement has been made can the Burnt Offering be presented to the Lord. The principle is clear enough for believers today. The word of Psalm 66.18 still remains, "If I regard iniquity in my heart, the Lord will not hear me" We must lift up "holy hands" when addressing God in prayer or worship. (1 Tim ch 2. v 8)

SINNING IN HOLY THINGS (Leviticus ch 5. vv 14-19)

How much this must have grieved the Lord, that the people whom He had redeemed should be negligent in holy things. To sin in things secular was grievous enough but to sin in holy things was especially sad. In this respect it is notable that sinning in holy things is now given a distinct and definite passage devoted entirely to that subject. But how may a man sin in holy things?

Adam Clarke explains admirably, "This law seems to relate particularly to sacrilege, and defrauds in spiritual matters; such as the neglect to consecrate or redeem the firstborn, the withholding of the first-fruits, tithes, and such like; and, according to the rabbins, making any secular gain of Divine things, keeping back any part of the price of things dedicated to God, or withholding what man had vowed to pay". The JFB Commentary adds "in eating of meats, which belonged to the priests alone". To this may be added, the failure to observe the Sabbath and other holy days, and neglect to keep the Feasts of the Lord at their appointed times. These all were sins in holy things which required an Offering of a particular kind and required also that restitution be made, and the value of such restitution be made by the priest who estimated the value according to the shekel of the sanctuary, the divine standard. There was too the requirement that a fifth part of that value be added to the principal.

But restitution and compensation would not make atonement. "The priest shall make an atonement for him with the ram".

There must be blood. "If a soul sin, and commit any of these things which are forbidden to be done by the commandments of the LORD; though he wist it not, yet is he guilty, and shall bear his iniquity. And he shall bring a ram without blemish out of the flock, with thy estimation, for a trespass offering, unto the priest: and the priest shall make an atonement for him concerning his ignorance wherein he erred and wist it not, and it shall be forgiven him. So has the Lord Jesus become our Sin Offering and has not only "restored that which He took not away" (Psalm 69. v 4), but has added a revenue of grace, so that both God and men are enriched immensely by the death of the Saviour.

Notice that "Trespass Offering", appearing in Leviticus ch 5. vv 15-19 occurs some four times in this short section. However, the Hebrew word here rendered "Trespass Offering" is the word *asham*, which according to Strong (817) means "guilt; guiltiness; sin offering; sin; trespass offering". In this difficult passage it may be better therefore to understand *asham* as "sin offering". This would be in keeping with that which has gone before and would preserve the contrast with what follows in chapter 6.

Christ in the Trespass Offering

Trespass and Sins

Reference has already been made to the difficulty of defining the difference between the Trespass Offering and the Sin Offering, and most expositors admit this difficulty. In chapter 4 there is no doubt or ambiguity for there the subject is the Sin Offering and this for sins of ignorance. From chapter 5. v 14 through into chapter 6 the emphasis is on the Trespass Offering and this for sins committed deliberately and knowingly. There is however, the recognition that sometimes there is an ignorance for which the transgressor is somewhat responsible, for perhaps he should have known. In which case, is this sinning ignorantly, or wilfully, or heedlessly, or otherwise? It has earlier been remarked that B.W.Newton refers to these cases as being "mediate", a sad mixture of ignorance and wilfulness and it is difficult to decide into which category to place these offences.

It is also pointed out by many that in chapter 4 the emphasis is on the person or persons and their state and condition, whereas in the verses mentioned in chapters 5 and 6 the emphasis is on the nature of the trespass.

How important to note that in both cases, whether the Sin Offering or the Trespass Offering it is distinctly stated that "it is most holy" (ch 6.v 25; ch 7. v 1). All sin is sin, whether committed ignorantly or otherwise, and requires the shedding of blood, and for us He who shed His blood was "most holy". Even when laden with sins, for which He suffered as a Substitute, He was personally and intrinsically holy. This the Father recognised so that, after the suffering He raised Him out from among the dead, His vicarious work completed.

Notice that sins committed against a neighbour are sins against the Lord. David recognised this, writing "Against thee, thee only, have I sinned, and done this evil in thy sight: that thou mightest be justified when thou speakest, and be clear when thou judgest" (Psalm 51. v 4). It might be argued that David's sin was against Uriah and his wife but since it was the law of the Lord that forbade the covetousness and adultery and murder of which David was guilty, then any violation of the law was an offence against the Lord who gave that law. Several instances of trespasses are now enumerated.

Lying (Lev ch 6. v 2)
This appears to envisage a case where a man has committed something to a neighbour to be kept for him. It may be goods or money or some living creatures as sheep or goats. The man does not keep an accurate record or obtain a receipt for that which he has deposited and when it comes time for him to recover his property there is a dispute. It is argued that the specific amount being claimed back was never really deposited and there is no proof available.

Again, as Adam Clarke suggests, "On the other hand, a man might accuse his neighbour of detaining property which had never been confided to him, or, after having been confided, had been restored again". It is one man's word against another's but some man has sinned and if this burdens his conscience sufficiently and is to be forgiven then there must be confession and an Offering.

Defrauding (Lev ch 6. v 2)
The word "fellowship" here is the Hebrew *tesoometh* (Strong 8667) and may indicate a business deal into which two persons have entered in partnership and have confirmed their deal by the "putting forth of the hand" which is the basic meaning of the word. Dr Gill explains, "as, for instance, having received money belonging to them both, denies he ever received any, and so cheats his partner of what was his due, and being put to his oath, takes it: or, "in putting of the hand", as persons usually

do when they enter into fellowship or partnership, they give each other their hand in token of it; or in putting anything into the hand, as money to trade with, and he denies he received any; or by way of purchase for anything bought, and the person of whom the purchase is made affirms the purchaser never put anything into his hand, or paid him anything, but insists upon being paid again"

There are so very many ways in which a man might have defrauded his neighbour and Dr Gill's summary is, "cheated him in trade and commerce, defrauded him in business, extorted money from him; or by calumny and false accusation got anything out of his hands, or by retaining the wages of the hireling"

Robbery by Violence (Lev ch 6. v 2)

The meaning here is clear enough except that some think that the said robbery was somehow done secretly and when challenged the offender denies the offence and swears falsely concerning it. But whether secretly or otherwise it was sin, which needed to be forgiven.

Stealing by Finding (Lev ch 6. v 3)

This is now the case where a man finds some lost thing. Of course he must know that this belongs to someone else and indeed he might even know the person to whom it belongs. However, he appropriates it to himself, making no enquiries and no effort to return that which he has found. This is theft. He is guilty. To compound the wrong he then denies stealing by finding and swears falsely concerning the matter.

Restoration, Compensation and an Offering. (Lev ch 6. vv4-6)

Notice that restoration and compensation must be attended to first, before an Offering is brought. This is to show the genuineness of the repentance, after which forgiveness may be sought. Verses 4-7 sum up so clearly just what is required of the offender seeking for forgiveness. "Then it shall be, because he hath sinned, and is guilty, that he shall restore that which he took violently away, or the thing which he hath deceitfully gotten, or that which was delivered him to keep, or the lost thing which he found. Or all that about which he hath sworn falsely; he shall even restore it in the principal, and shall add the fifth part more thereto, and give it unto him to whom it appertaineth, in the day of his trespass offering. And he shall bring his Trespass Offering unto the LORD, a ram without blemish out of the flock, with thy estimation, for a Trespass Offering, unto the priest: And the priest shall make an atonement for him before the LORD: and it shall be forgiven him for any thing of all that he hath done in trespassing therein".

The officiating priest was responsible for estimating, in shekels, the value of the goods in question (see Lev ch 5. vv15-16) and this was to be given to him who had been defrauded or deceived. But to this sum must be added a fifth part in compensation. Then the actual Offering was a ram without blemish, but since rams were of differing values this ram must be of a value commensurate with the value of the thing stolen. How accurately was this type fulfilled in our Lord Jesus. He was of course without blemish. There was no spot or blemish in Him and His blood was precious blood. There is no sin which it cannot cleanse.

How important to see that although confession, repentance and restitution were all necessary, yet not any of these, nor all of them, could atone for the sin. Without the shedding of blood there is no remission. The ram must be slain. As with certain other Offerings the fat and the hidden inward parts were to be burned on the altar. This was God's portion, an Offering made by fire. The priests may then eat the remaining flesh in the holy place, so sharing that which had already been offered to God. In this there was one law for the Sin Offering as for the Trespass Offering (Lev ch 7 v. 7). There is really no grading of sin. There may be degrees of responsibility and of privilege but all sin is equally grievous to the Lord. Again we are reminded that the Offering is "most holy" (Lev ch 7 v. 6). So was our Sinless Substitute. Even when bearing the sins which Jehovah had laid upon Him He was essentially holy (Isaiah ch 53 v. 6).

The Consecration of the Priests

The Priesthood Consecrated

Those must have been memorable days when Aaron and his sons were consecrated for their priestly ministry. Heavy duties lay ahead for the priestly family and it was essential that the people should observe the ceremony which set the family apart for God. The consecrated priesthood was to function in an intermediary way between Jehovah and the people and the congregation must see that this was by divine decree, and was not a domestic arrangement between Moses and Aaron. Accordingly we read, "and the assembly was gathered together unto the door of the tabernacle of the congregation. And Moses said unto the congregation, This is the thing which the LORD commanded to be done" (Lev ch 8. vv 4-5). The court of course would not be large enough to contain the whole congregation so doubtless the elders of the tribes would take first place and when the court was filled it is likely that many of the people would assemble on surrounding hillsides to view the great event. Again, as the consecration ceremonies were to be repeated daily for seven days it may be that some of the people would view on one day and others on another day. It was indeed important that all should witness this inauguration of the priesthood.

All the sons of Aaron and their descendants were priests by birth but it was only after this consecration that they were able to function in priestly ministry. The searching question must then be asked whether, though all believers in the Lord Jesus are priests by birth, do we all, as a royal and holy priesthood rise to our responsibility to exercise a consecrated priestly ministry among, and for, the saints?

The Preparation

In preparation for the consecrations Moses brought Aaron and his sons, probably to the laver, and washed them with water. Those who handle divine things and minister in holy matters must themselves be clean. The washing is typical of the purity required in saints today. Our Great High Priest is of course essentially and personally pure. "Such an High Priest became us, who is holy, harmless, undefiled, separate from sinners" (Heb ch 7. v 26). Aaron and his sons were now bathed entirely and not just hands and feet as it would be in their later ministrations.

Upon Aaron, now suitably cleansed, Moses put the High Priestly garments. The verses concerned (Lev ch 8. vv 7-9) are self-explanatory but the garments are described more fully in Exodus ch 28. vv 4-39. As the people watched, "He put upon him the coat, and girded him with the girdle, and clothed him with the robe, and put the ephod upon him, and he girded him with the curious girdle of the ephod, and bound it unto him therewith. And he put the breastplate upon him: also he put in the breastplate the Urim and the Thummim. And he put the mitre upon his head; also upon the mitre, even upon his forefront, did he put the golden plate, the holy crown; as the LORD commanded Moses". These were the garments for glory and beauty that made Aaron the high priest distinct from his sons the priests. What a sight indeed he must have been when so dressed in his high priestly garments. So is our blessed Lord distinct and supreme among His saints.

The Anointing Oil

Having been appropriately washed and dressed Aaron must now be anointed with oil, but first the oil must be used to sanctify the tabernacle and all that was therein. "And Moses took the anointing oil, and anointed the tabernacle and all that was therein, and sanctified them. And he sprinkled thereof upon the altar seven times, and anointed the altar and all his vessels, both the laver and his foot, to sanctify them". Reference to the vessels, which would be pans, shovels, basins, flesh hooks, firepans, would seem to indicate that this is the altar of Burnt Offering, and since the laver is also mentioned it does appear that the vessels and furniture in the court were all sanctified, as well perhaps as the vessels in the holy place. After this the oil was poured upon Aaron. So is our Lord Jesus "anointed with the oil of gladness above His fellows" (Psalm 45. v 7).

Following this Moses now brought Aaron's sons, Nadab and Abihu, Eleazar and Ithamar, and clothed them with coats, girdles and bonnets.

However, all ministry of the sanctuary and all access to the Divine Presence must be based upon sacrifice and it is now that the Offerings are introduced. There must be a Sin Offering, and for this purpose a bullock had been brought (Lev chapter 8 v. 2). Albert Barnes has an interesting comment and writes, "The Sin Offering was now offered for the first time. The succession in which the Offerings followed each other on this occasion, first the Sin Offering, then the Burnt Offering, and lastly the Peace Offering, has its ground in the meaning of each sacrifice ... The worshipper passed through a spiritual process. He had transgressed the law and he needed the atonement signified by the Sin Offering; if his Offering had been made in truth and sincerity, he could then offer himself as an accepted person, as a sweet savour, in the Burnt Offering; and in consequence he could enjoy communion with the Lord and with his brethren in the Peace Offering"

Aaron and his sons had laid their hands on the head of the bullock, signifying their identification with it, and now they similarly lay their hands on the head of the ram for the Burnt Offering. The slain ram was cut into pieces and the ritual prescribed in Leviticus chapter 1 was now followed.

The second ram is called "the ram of consecration". It was killed and its blood was applied by Moses upon the right ear, the thumb of the right hand and the great toe of the right foot of each priest. This ritual applied alike to Aaron and to his sons. The priestly family was accordingly consecrated by blood to the priesthood, and the altar too, sprinkled with blood was similarly sanctified. The blood upon the extremities signified the fitness and readiness of the priests to hear and to do whatever Jehovah commanded.

It will be remembered that there was also a basket of unleavened bread. Out of this basket Moses took various portions of the bread and took also several prescribed pieces of the slain ram of consecration. With these he filled the hands of Aaron and his sons. What they now had in their hands was waved as a wave offering before the Lord. He must observe first what was being offered. It may well have been, as Jewish tradition has it, that Moses put his own hands under the hands of the priests and so moved their hands from left to right, to and fro, thus creating the wave offering. It was an impressive sight watched by the people. Moses then took what had been waved from the hands of the priests and offered all upon the altar of Burnt Offering as a sweet savour. Sweet indeed it was to Jehovah that there was now a consecrated priestly family to assist the people in their service and worship.

Aaron and his sons were now anointed with the oil. Note that this was not the ordinary olive oil which was used on many other occasions. It was the holy anointing oil prepared as in Exodus ch 30. vv 23-25. "Take thou also unto thee principal spices, of pure myrrh five hundred shekels, and of sweet cinnamon half so much, even two hundred and fifty shekels, and of sweet calamus two hundred and fifty shekels, And of cassia five hundred shekels, after the shekel of the sanctuary, and of oil olive an hin: And thou shalt make it an oil of holy ointment, an ointment compound after the art of the apothecary: it shall be an holy anointing oil".

This chapter is in the main self-explanatory. It should be read carefully and prayerfully, followed by the directions for the eighth day ceremony which brought the inauguration ritual to a close in chapter 9. For seven days the priestly family had been commanded to abide in the court and the consecration ritual was repeated daily. They were not to go outside the precincts of the tabernacle, but then, on the eighth day there was a series of Offerings and the day ended with "And Aaron lifted up his hand toward the people, and blessed them, and came down from offering of the Sin Offering, and the Burnt Offering, and Peace Offerings. And Moses and Aaron went into the tabernacle of the congregation, and came out, and blessed the people: and the glory of the LORD appeared unto all the people. And there came a fire out from before the LORD, and consumed upon the altar the Burnt Offering and the fat, which, when all the people saw, they shouted, and fell on their faces".

The eighth day is full of significance for believers today. It is the first day of the week. For us it is the Lord's Day. It is the day of resurrection and joy, full of memories of Him who offered Himself without spot to God and is now in glory, exalted far above all. We worship, and meanwhile await His return.

Leviticus ch 16. vv 2-34; ch 23. vv 26-32

The Day of Atonement

Yom Kippur

Although the Day of Atonement is more often associated with the Feasts of the Lord in Leviticus ch 23 rather than with the Offerings of the early chapters, yet it seems fitting to include the study here since several of the Offerings mentioned earlier were involved during that great Day. The day is known among Jewish people by the Hebrew title *Yom Kippur*, which means "the day of covering". It was, and is still, the greatest day in the Hebrew Calendar, and is observed always on the tenth day of the month *Tishrei* which is the first month of the Jewish civil year but the seventh month of the ecclesiastical year, answering to our September/October. The title is actually in the plural, literally the Day of Atonements, but this may be the Hebrew plurality which signifies the greatness of the Day, for it was on that Day that the greatest expiation that could be known under the Old Covenant took place for the nation. Some however, take the plurality literally and understand that the Day of Atonement foretold typically that in the death of Christ there was atonement for Israel, for the Church and for the world. (1 John ch 2. v 2).

It was after the untimely death, in divine judgment, of Aaron's two sons Nadab and Abihu, that the Day of Atonement was instituted to teach Israel that man could not, in his own way, approach God. Nadab and Abihu had dared to approach in a manner not commanded by the Lord and fire from the Lord devoured them. (Leviticus ch 10. vv 1-2.). After this there were then clear and strict instructions given regarding access by the High Priest into the sanctuary in a way approved by the Lord.

The Offerings

On this memorable Day of Atonement one bullock, two rams, and two goats were offered as Sin Offerings and Burnt Offerings, each in its own time and place during the Day, as prescribed by the Lord.

The Day began with the presentation by Aaron of a young bullock for a Sin Offering and a ram for a Burnt Offering. He then took from the congregation two goats for a Sin Offering and a ram for a Burnt Offering.

Having washed his flesh in water Aaron then girded himself with the linen garments, the coat, the breeches, the girdle and the mitre. These all spoke of holiness. Some types are types of contrast, and here we must remember that our great High Priest, the Lord Jesus, did not need cleansing, but was always holy, and as such enjoyed unbroken communion with His Father. Aaron and his house needed atonement and so he first offered the young bullock for a Sin Offering, another contrasting type, for the Saviour needed no such Offering for Himself.

Sweet Incense

It is to be noted however, that when Aaron first entered the holiest the directions were clear. He must approach with "a censer full of burning coals of fire from off the altar before the LORD, and his hands full of sweet incense beaten small, and bring it within the veil: And he shall put the incense upon the fire before the LORD, that the cloud of the incense may cover the mercy seat that is upon the testimony, that he die not". Aaron entered into the holiest covered with an incense cloud typical of that sweet and sinless perfection in which our Lord Jesus went into death for us whom He represented. (Lev ch 16. vv12-13).

The Blood

Aaron killed the bullock, the Sin Offering for himself and his house, and with his finger he sprinkled its blood upon the mercy seat eastward, and seven times before the mercy seat. Thus Jehovah was satisfied with the atonement for Aaron and his house.

Meanwhile, lots had been cast upon the two goats. One would be slain and the other led into the wilderness to die there laden with the sins of the people. The blood of the slain goat, Sin Offering for the people, was then to be sprinkled on and before the mercy seat just as the blood of the bullock had been. The very tabernacle itself had been defiled by the sins of the people and needed atonement. As John Wesley writes, "For though the people did not enter into that place, yet their sins entered thither, and would hinder the effects of the high priest's mediation on their behalf if God was not reconciled to them ... a sinful people, who defile not themselves only, but also God's sanctuary. And God hereby shewed them, how much their hearts needed to be purified, when even the tabernacle, only by standing in the midst of them, needed this expiation". The tabernacle would indeed remain in the midst of them but needed atonement because of the sins of the people.

Coming out of the holiest into the holy place Aaron would now take of the blood of the bullock and the blood of the goat and sprinkle this seven times on the horns of the golden altar of incense, which is here called "the altar that is before the Lord" for indeed it stood just before the veil, behind which Jehovah dwelt between the cherubim. (Lev ch 16. v 18).

Azazel!

The remaining goat was a scapegoat. *Azazel* is the Hebrew word for "scapegoat" (Strong 5799), and means literally, "the goat of departure". This goat would now be led, by the hand of a fit man, with the iniquities of the congregation confessed upon it by the high priest, into the wilderness. Many legends and speculations have grown up about the eventual fate of the scapegoat but it is enough to know that somewhere, in a land uninhabited, the goat would die, in type laden with the sins of the people. The story of the scapegoat has been beautifully written in verse, part of which is –

> I saw a land, a solitary land,
> A land from every other land afar.
> No sun had ever kissed the gloomy strand,
> Nor dawn, nor day, nor moon, nor morning star.
>
> I saw a goat with heavy head drooped low,
> With sunken eye, and worn, far-travelled feet;
> In that sad land alone, a living woe,
> I heard its hoarse, forsaken, piteous bleat.
>
> It pierced the moral universe on high,
> Upon eternal shores the echoes brake,
> That loud, that lone, that lamentable cry;
> My God, My God, Why didst Thou Me forsake?
>
> I.Y.Ewan

The Final Service

Having completed the service of the inner sanctuary Aaron now put off the linen garments, leaving them in the holy place. He then washed himself in water in the holy place, put on his high priestly garments and came out to the court where there were yet two Offerings to be attended to. The ram for the Burnt Offering for himself and the ram for the Burnt Offering for the congregation were then to be offered in the manner prescribed in the law of the Offerings. Only after Jehovah had been propitiated with the Sin Offerings could He be approached with Burnt Offerings

The fat of the Sin Offerings was then to be burned on the brazen altar in the court, but the carcases of those Sin Offerings whose blood had been carried into the sanctuary must now be carried outside the camp and burned in totality, their skins, their flesh and their dung. The man who burned them must wash his clothes and bathe his flesh in water, and only then come again into the camp. This stipulation applied likewise to the man who had led the scapegoat into the wilderness.

The Interpretation of the Type.

It is to be hoped that this great type needs little in the way of explanation. Here plainly foreshadowed is the glory of One who was both Sin Offering and Burnt Offering for His people. In absolute personal holiness He went to Golgotha as a sinless Substitute and having suffered what men could see as He hung on the cross He then went alone into the land uninhabited, forsaken of God. He has made a full atonement. He has satisfied God, "And he shall make an atonement for the holy sanctuary, and he shall make an atonement for the tabernacle of the congregation, and for the altar, and he shall make an atonement for the priests, and for all the people of the congregation". As it was with Aaron so it was with the son who would succeed him, and with his son after that, "to make an atonement for the children of Israel for all their sins once a year" (Lev ch 16. v 34). This of course was every year, but how blessed it is for us to read of the Lord Jesus that "by his own blood he entered in once into the holy place, having obtained eternal redemption for us" (Heb ch 9. v 12). The work of Christ will never need to be repeated. God is eternally satisfied, as are those who trust the Saviour.

(Leviticus ch 14)

The Cleansing of the Leper

The Condition

It must be well known that leprosy is a foul disease. Dr W. M. Thompson in his excellent work "The Land and the Book" says that when fully developed it turns a man into "a mass of loathsomeness" and there can be little doubt that leprosy is, in so many respects, typical of sin. Like sin, it begins insidiously, it disfigures a man, it renders him unsociable, and if not dealt with it will result in death. Leprosy affected a man's person, his garments, and his house, and so does sin. Perhaps initially these chapters concerning the leper and his cleansing will teach us the heinousness of sin and the necessity for cleansing.

It was the responsibility of the priest to follow the detailed directions given in chapter 13 to diagnose the plague in a man. In the early stages the symptoms may have looked quite like a boil but it would have been a tragedy if a leper's disease had been treated as if it were just a boil. On the other hand it would have been equally tragic if the poor sufferer should be pronounced leprous when his problem was as simple as a boil. So the priest was indeed very responsible to arrive at a correct diagnosis and the instructions of chapter 13 were intended for his guidance. When once the man had been pronounced leprous he was unclean. He must then leave the camp since the condition was contagious. His separation from the congregation prevented, in some measure, the contamination of others. Leprosy therefore made the man a lonely man and indeed someone to be avoided. "And the leper in whom the plague is, his clothes shall be rent, and his head bare, and he shall put a covering upon his upper lip, and shall cry, Unclean, unclean. All the days wherein the plague shall be in him he shall be defiled; he is unclean: he shall dwell alone; without the camp shall his habitation be" (Lev ch 13. vv 45-46). What a humiliation this must have been and what a picture of a sinner convicted of his awful condition and his great need!

But at least there was hope, and this was very much dependent on the priest, who had to go forth out of the camp to meet the infected man. It is now that the required Offerings are introduced, "two birds alive and clean, and with them cedar wood, scarlet, and hyssop". We shall meet these latter items in our consideration of the Red Heifer, and Newberry comments, "The typical import of the cedar wood, the worm scarlet, and the hyssop is best explained by Phil ch2. vv 6-8. The CEDAR WOOD is significant of HIGHEST DIGNITY, the HYSSOP that grows on the wall of DEEPEST HUMILIATION, and the WORM SCARLET of the EARTHLY DIGNITY of the Son of Man who was born of the seed of David, who in the form of God and of the Royal line of David humbled Himself even to the death of the cross". (*Capitals are Newberry's*).

The Cleansing

Note that when in due course the leper has been pronounced clean by the priest he must be cleansed publicly from anything of the old leprous life so that he might take his place again in the camp and among his people, and there follows "the law of the cleansing".

The two birds referred to are, in the Hebrew, *tsippor* (Strong 6833) which signifies "a little bird or sparrow". In the market place these were of course, practically worthless. As the Saviour Himself said, "Are not two sparrows sold for a farthing?" It seems that the Lord will not make the desired cleansing difficult or out of reach for the poorest of His people. And do not "little birds" typify the humility of the Lord Jesus and His apparent weakness in the eyes of men? Some commentators do follow the Septuagint rendering "little birds" and suggest that these could have been doves or pigeons but this does not affect the typical teaching.

The priest then commanded that one of the birds should be killed over an earthen vessel and in running or "living" water. Whether another priest would do this, or some other person, is not clear, but as water is often a symbol of the Holy Spirit some have seen here an ancient picture of that verse in Hebrews ch 9. v 14, "Christ, who through the eternal Spirit offered himself without spot to God". Then again, as the blood would mingle with the water some have been reminded, with some justification, of the blood and water that flowed from the wounded side of the Saviour (John ch 19. v 34).

In some way then the hyssop was wrapped around the cedar wood. Was it with scarlet wool? This would have formed a kind of bundle with a cedar wood handle and then this would be dipped in the blood and water. The blood was first sprinkled seven times on the leper himself, after which the living bird, having been dipped in the blood, was released to soar into the air. It would rise into the heavens carrying the sprinkled blood with it. What a foreshadowing this is of the Saviour, going down into death and then rising and ascending into the heavens (Heb ch 9. v 24). "By his own blood he entered in once into the holy place, having obtained eternal redemption for us". To quote Newberry again, "His divine glory, human excellency, and lowly obedience unto death giving their united value to His atoning work". Typically, the pardoned sinner is now "clean", and the believer today enjoys that word "The blood of Jesus Christ cleanseth us from all sin".

It was now incumbent upon the cleansed leper that he should give visual evidence of his cleansing, so after seven days he must wash his clothes and his flesh and shave off his hair. Garments in Scripture are often typical of character and the man now manifests an outward change by his washed clothing. Things are different now! The shaving off of the hair may signify a renunciation of that which is natural and it is easy to see how all this is so relevant to those who confess Christ. They are new creatures now, with new appearances, new demeanour, new habits and new desires, known and recognised as those who have been cleansed and are now identified with the Crucified but Risen Saviour.

The eighth day was then a most significant day in the experience of the cleansed leper. The number "8" is the number of a new beginning. After seven days in the week the eighth day begins anew, another week. After seven notes of music in the scale the eighth is a new beginning. Seven colours in the rainbow complete the splendour of the bow and the eighth is again a new beginning. The eighth day is therefore akin to the first day and it was on this first, or eighth day that our Lord rose from the dead.

On this eighth day the leper was required to bring "two he lambs without blemish, and one ewe lamb of the first year without blemish, and three tenth deals of fine flour for a meat offering, mingled with oil, and one log of oil". The priest would then bring the man, with his Offerings, to the door of the tabernacle, and present him before the Lord. How like the ministry of our Great High Priest! Forgiven sinners are now, in Christ, brought into the very presence of God, but at what a cost! These Offerings were to be offered as a Trespass Offering, a Burnt Offering, a Sin Offering and a Meat Offering, with the oil applied both to the Offerings and to the man himself as prescribed. What a remembrance of Calvary!

But yet again it is acknowledged that there were poor of the people who could not bring the required Offerings and Jehovah graciously meets such in their poverty. "And if he be poor, and cannot get so much; then he shall take one lamb for a trespass offering to be waved, to make an atonement for him, and one tenth deal of fine flour mingled with oil for a meat offering, and a log of oil; and two turtledoves, or two young pigeons, such as he is able to get; and the one shall be a sin offering, and the other a burnt offering. And he shall bring them on the eighth day for his cleansing unto the priest, unto the door of the tabernacle of the congregation, before the LORD". (Lev ch 14. vv 21-24).

For the believer today the lesson is clear. By the work of our High Priest, the value of the precious blood shed, and the ministry of the Holy Spirit, we are now freely able to enter the holiest. God is satisfied; sins are forgiven; the Spirit has been given; we are accepted in the Beloved and welcomed as worshippers into the Divine presence.

Matthew Henry comments on this passage, "We have here the gracious provision which the law made for the cleansing of poor lepers. If they were not able to bring three lambs, and three tenth-deals of flour, they must bring one lamb, and one tenth-deal of flour, and, instead of the other two lambs, two turtle-doves or two young pigeons ... The poverty of the person concerned would not excuse him if he brought no offering at all ... God expected from those who were poor only according to their ability; his commandments are not grievous ... The poor are as welcome to God's altar as the rich; and, if there be first a willing mind and an honest heart, two pigeons, when they are the utmost a man is able to get, are as acceptable to God as two lambs; for he requires according to what a man has and not according to what he has not. But it is observable that though a meaner sacrifice was accepted from the poor, yet the very same ceremony was used for them as was for the rich; for their souls are as precious and Christ and his gospel are the same to both".

Many there are today whose comprehension and apprehension of the work of the Cross may be very limited, but our cleansing and acceptance before God is not dependent upon our knowledge. It is God's estimate of Christ and Calvary which assures our salvation. Simple faith brings the poorest and weakest into the joy of it.

What a change the cleansing of the leper made, in the man, in his garments, and even in his house. There follows the case where, when they were come into the land, the plague may indeed be found in the house. The directions are clear and explicit; the examination must be rigorous until cleansing is effected. So it is today. How does faith in Christ affect a man's person and family and house, until friends and neighbours see and know that something indeed has happened to the man, and who can tell what might be wrought by his testimony to the Saviour?

(Leviticus ch 23. vv 13, 18, 37)

The Drink Offering

The First Mention

Although there are more than fifty references to the Drink Offering in our Bible and although it is so often included for meditation with the Levitical Offerings, yet the above are the only three references in the Book of Leviticus and they are all in close proximity in chapter 23. The first mention of a Drink Offering is in Genesis ch 35. v 14 and remembering "the law of the first mention" perhaps it is here that we find, at least in embryo, the purpose and meaning of the Drink Offering.

Jacob is as renowned for rearing pillars as his father Isaac was renowned for digging wells and his grandfather Abraham for pitching tents. In this instance, in Genesis ch 35, Jacob had just had a memorable meeting with the Lord at Bethel. Jehovah had appeared to him as *El Shaddai*, God Almighty, (Strong 7703). God had blessed Jacob and had repeated promises to him concerning his seed and a land, and Jacob set up his pillar to commemorate the great event. He confirmed the name Bethel, poured wine upon his monumental pillar and anointed it with oil. Then, after a very few references in the Book of Exodus the Drink Offering is only mentioned in association with the Burnt Offerings and Peace Offerings as prescribed in the Book of Leviticus. The Hebrew word for Drink Offering is *nehsek* (Strong 5262) meaning simply "a libation". Adam Clarke says of the Drink Offerings, "At first they consisted probably of water only, afterwards wine was used. The pillar which Jacob set up was to commemorate the appearance of God to him; the drink-offering and the oil were intended to express his gratitude and devotion to his Preserver". The thought has been expressed by some writers that there may have been a Drink Offering involved in Genesis ch 14. v 18 in the case of Melchizedek's meeting with Abraham. Melchizedek brought forth bread and wine but there is really no mention or suggestion of a Drink Offering.

The Hebrew word *nehsek* is first used of Drink Offerings in general and even of those that had been poured out as Offerings to false gods (Jer ch 32. v 29), but with the introduction of the Levitical system *nehsek* is used to denote the libation which was poured on the Burnt Offerings and Peace Offerings in association with Meat Offerings, all of which were sweet-savour Offerings. The Meat Offering and the Drink Offering were accompanying Offerings, often called subsidiary, but this term must not imply that they were of lesser value or importance. Typically they are very beautiful as has already been observed in the study of the Meat Offering.

THE ELEMENTS
Oil
These elements were intended typically to express joy and gratitude. There was gratitude on the part of the offerer and there was joy for both God and the offerer. Jacob poured oil on his pillar as a Drink Offering and as has been noticed in the study of the Meat Offering in Leviticus 2 oil is a fitting symbol of fullness and fatness, an abundance of blessing particularly through the ministry of the Holy Spirit. So by that same Spirit today's believers have come to appreciate Christ and it is the believer's privilege to pour out that appreciation to God like a Drink Offering, rejoicing in the fullness of what Christ means to God, and to His people.

Water
It will be remembered that David once poured out a libation of water to the Lord in appreciation and gratitude. David, in exile, had longed for a drink of the water of the well of Bethlehem, the town of his birth and boyhood. Three of his loyal men endangered their own lives and broke through the ranks of the Philistines to obtain that water, but when they brought it to David he could not drink it. It was emblematic of the lives of those

men who had risked life and limb to get it for him. He poured it out unto the Lord (2 Sam ch 23.vv 15-16). As it is recorded "David longed, and said, Oh that one would give me drink of the water of the well of Bethlehem, which is by the gate! And the three mighty men brake through the host of the Philistines, and drew water out of the well of Bethlehem, that was by the gate, and took it, and brought it to David: nevertheless he would not drink thereof, but poured it out unto the LORD". So do we who love the Saviour pour out our expressions of gratitude for One who not only endangered His life but willingly gave it for us.

Wine

Wine was explicitly prescribed for the Drink Offering in Exodus ch 29. v 40. It is said of it, "Wine that maketh glad the heart of man" (Psalm 104 v 15). It is a symbol of joy and was the accompanying Drink Offering of the continual Burnt Offering when two yearling lambs were offered daily, one every morning and one every evening. "Now this is that which thou shalt offer upon the altar; two lambs of the first year day by day continually. The one lamb thou shalt offer in the morning; and the other lamb thou shalt offer at even: And with the one lamb a tenth deal of flour mingled with the fourth part of an hin of beaten oil; and the fourth part of an hin of wine for a Drink Offering. And the other lamb thou shalt offer at even, and shalt do thereto according to the Meat Offering of the morning, and according to the Drink Offering thereof, for a sweet savour, an offering made by fire unto the LORD. This shall be a continual Burnt Offering throughout your generations" (Exod ch 29 vv 38-42)

With the lamb of the Burnt Offering, which was wholly for God, were offered the Meat Offering and the Drink Offering of wine. What a treasury of symbols! Death in the offered lamb of the Burnt Offering. Life in the fine flour of the Meat Offering. Joy in the poured out wine of the Drink Offering. What a pattern for our weekly remembrance meeting. Memories of the death of Christ. Memories of His lovely Life. God's joy and ours as we bring these memories to the Father, pouring out our feelings for Him as best we can.

Christ and the Drink Offering

In the well-known and much loved Isaiah 53 we read of the Saviour, "He hath poured out his soul unto death" (v.12). Our Lord's entire life was poured out for others in lowly service. He came, not to be ministered unto but to minister (Matt ch 20.v 28). This He did for the blessing of others and for the glory of His Father, and in it all He had the greatest joy. Eventually His life was poured out in the death of the cross. What a delightful study it is to read of the joy and rejoicing of the Man of Sorrows. Even at Calvary He could despise the shame for the joy that was set before Him (Heb ch 12. v 2).

Paul and the Drink Offering

The same symbolism is used of the devoted ministry of Paul. He esteemed the sacrifice and service of the Philippians as a Burnt Offering and could say that he was being offered upon that sacrifice as a Drink Offering. The word which he uses is *spendo* (Strong 4689) which means "to pour out as a libation" and so does JND translate Philippians ch 2.v 17, "But if also I am poured out as a libation on the sacrifice and ministration of your faith, I rejoice, and rejoice in common with you all". Elsewhere the word *spendo* occurs only in 2 Timothy ch 4. v 6 where Paul uses it to describe the literal pouring out of his life in imminent death. Like his Lord, in life and in death Paul was poured out as a libation. Notice his joy in it too. It was indeed a real Drink Offering, whether living or dying poured out with joy.

The Believer and the Drink Offering

While the Drink Offering is not specifically mentioned, perhaps that great exhortation of Romans ch 12. v 1 is akin to the pouring out of our lives in gratitude for the mercies of God. "I beseech you therefore, brethren, by the mercies of God, that ye present your bodies a living sacrifice, holy, acceptable unto God, which is your reasonable service". It is the appeal of one who himself had presented himself as a living sacrifice, even unto death. May we have grace to follow his example.

Numbers ch 19. vv 1-22

The Red Heifer

The Purpose

As with the Day of Atonement the ordinance of the Red Heifer does not strictly belong to the Levitical Offerings. Nevertheless, there is a victim, there is the shedding and sprinkling of blood, and the twice used expression "Sin Offering" (Num ch 19. vv 9,17), Hebrew *chatta'ah* (Strong 2403), which all seems to justify its inclusion in a study of the Offerings. Being called an ordinance, and being found only in the Book of Numbers, the Book of the wilderness, the Red Heifer appears to be concerned with defilement along the way. Defilement may so often have been contracted unintentionally and unavoidably, as for instance when one may have been present in a tent when a man died. Such close contact with death constituted a person unclean and so he required the cleansing which the Red Heifer provided. The ordinance had to do with defilement of the ceremonial kind rather than with that which was moral. As Hebrews ch 9. v 13 points out, it was concerned with the purifying of the flesh.

The Criteria (v.2)

Notice that the Heifer was provided by the congregation. It was not, initially, a personal exercise, but of general application. It is not clear how the whole congregation was to provide one Heifer but so it was. There were strict criteria regarding the victim. It was female of course, and it was to be red in colour. It must be a healthy animal with no spot, and with no mixture of another colour. Should there be found in it a hair of another colour the animal would be rejected. Nor must it have any defect or deformity. It must never have borne a yoke, never been used for any common agricultural purpose. In these criteria there is at once a clear type of the Lord Jesus. As has been seen again and again in the other Offerings the Saviour was without blemish. If at times in those Offerings He had the strong characteristics of the active male, so also had He the patient submissiveness of the passive female, and He never was, at any time, the Servant of men, though He served men as no other man ever did.

The word "red" is the Hebrew word *adom* (Strong 122), akin to the name of the first man, Adam, the man of the ground. Is there here an early reminder of the real humanity of the Lord Jesus. In great grace and voluntary humility He became, in Manhood, what He had never been before so that He might accomplish that atoning work of which believers are now the joyful beneficiaries.

The Procedure (vv 3-6)

Although the Heifer was initially brought to Moses and Aaron they were now instructed to give it to Eleazar. He was a priest, one of the sons of Aaron, but the question arises as to why Aaron himself did not attend to the required duties. It would seem that the High Priest was to be preserved from the defilement which was necessarily involved, even though it was a temporary ceremonial defilement.

Eleazar was then to take the Heifer and lead it outside the camp to be slain "before his face". Whether Eleazar or another would kill the Heifer is not clear. It would appear, as a consensus of other translations would indicate, that it was indeed some person other than Eleazar who was delegated to kill the Heifer. "One shall slaughter it before him" (JND). "One shall slay her before his face" (ASV). "It shall be slaughtered before him" (RSV). Many other versions also suggest that while Eleazar supervised the slaughter it was actually carried out by another.

Note that very important direction however, that it was "outside the camp" that the animal was slain, and burned. "Her skin, and her flesh, and her blood, with her dung, shall he burn" And so the Epistle to the Hebrews states, "Wherefore Jesus also, that he might sanctify the people with his own blood, suffered without the gate" (Heb ch 13. v 12). How accurately were the types fulfilled. Golgotha was indeed outside the walls of Jerusalem, outside the camp, and there Jesus suffered and died.

Eleazar the priest then took up his priestly duties. Comparing what follows with the Sin Offering of Leviticus ch 4 v. 17 it would seem that Eleazar must have carried at least a portion of the blood in a basin until he was near the Tabernacle. Then he would dip his finger in the blood and sprinkle it seven times directly before the tent of meeting. As the JFB Commentary suggests, "By this attitude he indicated that he was presenting an expiatory sacrifice, for the acceptance of which he hoped, in the grace of God, by looking to the mercy seat". "Seven times" implied the completeness of the sacrifice and so the remaining duties could now be attended to.

Apart from the blood which was sprinkled, the Heifer, in its entirety, was now to be burned in the sight of Eleazar the priest. As has already been quoted, "Her skin, and her flesh, and her blood, with her dung, shall he burn" (v.5). Then, into the midst of the burning, Eleazar was to cast cedar wood, hyssop, and scarlet. Note that these were also used in the cleansing of the unclean leper (Lev ch 14. v 4). Commentators differ as to the interpretation of the cedar wood, hyssop and scarlet, but there does seem to be a typical connection with that true and holy manhood of the Lord Jesus which has already been noted. Solomon noted the extremes when it was written of him "And he spake of trees, from the cedar tree that is in Lebanon even unto the hyssop that springeth out of the wall" (1 Kings ch 4. v 33).

The majestic cedar was typical of the highest point, the very zenith of true humanity, but the humble hyssop, growing out of the wall, indicated humility in the extreme, while the scarlet in its glory links the two. In the Saviour we see the majesty of His unique and pure humanity; and likewise we see that lowliness which He exhibited during the whole of His lovely life, from the manger to the cross. The glory of a perfect humanity is displayed in Him wherever we view Him. If it be objected that this interpretation of the type cannot be, since the cedar wood, hyssop, and scarlet were cast into the burning, typical of the judgment of God, this objection is not valid. Our Lord Jesus, the epitome of true, real, holy Manhood did indeed endure the judgment of God against sin. Of course He Himself had no sin, but for us He endured that judgment of which Paul writes "For He hath made him to be sin for us, who knew no sin; that we might be made the righteousness of God in Him" (2 Cor ch 5. v 21).

The Preparation of the Ashes (vv 7-10)

The ashes of the heifer are mentioned in the Epistle to the Hebrews (ch 9. v 13). They are most important. The priest who attended to these duties must now wash his clothes and bathe his flesh in water and only then was he permitted to come back into the camp. Even then he was ceremonially unclean until the evening. The same applied to the man who burned the heifer. He then who gathered up the ashes was also reckoned to be unclean and must, like the others involved, wash his clothes and bathe his flesh in water and be unclean until the even.

The man who gathered up the ashes was now to lay them up in a clean place outside the camp. How exactly was this type fulfilled in the Saviour. Having died outside the camp His holy body was taken down from the cross by the hands of a clean person, Joseph of Arimathaea. He was indeed a clean person, a good man (Luke), an honourable man (Mark), who begged the Body of Jesus, took it down and laid it in a sepulchre which, like the cross, was also outside the city. "Now in the place where he was crucified there was a garden; and in the garden a new sepulchre, wherein was never man yet laid. There laid they Jesus therefore" (John ch 19. vv 41-42). A clean person and a clean place fulfilled the ancient type.

The Purpose of the Ashes (vv 11-22)

It has earlier been remarked that the ashes of the Red Heifer were for the cleansing of a man defiled by death. The ordinance was for the children of Israel and also for the stranger who sojourned among them. A defiled person defiled the camp and therefore must be cleansed. So it is with believers today. Our salvation is not in question. That is settled for ever. But salvation is one thing, sanctification is another. It is a defiled and defiling world through which the people of God pass. In such a variety of ways the saintliest of men can be defiled and a man with unconfessed defilement will readily defile the assembly of which he forms a part. It was of course inevitable that with such a large congregation there must have been recurring deaths in their tents. Whoever touched the dead person was unclean for seven days and this applied also to all who came into the tent and everything that was in the tent. How contagious is defilement! As v.22 states, "whatsoever the unclean person toucheth shall be unclean; and the soul that toucheth it shall be unclean". Every open uncovered vessel in the tent was likewise defiled. Touching the corpse of a man who had died in the open field also brought defilement, and even touching a bone or a grave defiled a man too.

For such uncleanness running water was to be caught in a vessel with some of the ashes of the Heifer sprinkled upon it. A clean person should then take a bunch of hyssop, dip it in the water and sprinkle it upon the tent, the vessels, and all the persons associated with the defilement. The clean person shall do this on the third day and repeat it on the seventh day, the two numbers "3" and "7" signifying completeness or perfection. After this the clean person who had attended to the sprinkling must purify himself by washing his clothes and bathing in water. Those who seek, albeit in all sincerity, to restore a fallen brother, must be so careful about their own condition. "Brethren, if a man be overtaken in a fault, ye which are spiritual, restore such an one in the spirit of meekness; considering thyself, lest thou also be tempted" (Gal 6.1).

The water was called the water of separation, or sanctification, and it was so important that if a man was unclean and neglected to be cleansed by it he would be cut off from the congregation.

So it is today, that sin not confessed and dealt with, can, sadly, result in the putting away of that person from the assembly, by excommunication as in 1 Corinthians ch.5 v 13 or even in God's governmental judgment as in 1 Corinthians ch 11. v 30.

The ashes of the Heifer were the memorial of the burning. So the remembrance of Calvary should keep us clean. The Saviour suffered so much to sanctify a people for Himself. How grievous it must be to Him when His people are defiled by the very world which nailed Him to the tree.

As J. Stubbs writes, so fittingly, "The message of this so practical chapter in Numbers is clear and searching. Sin in God's eye is a most defiling thing. God is supreme and absolute in His holiness and therefore He will not allow sin in His presence. Sin, unless dealt with in the life and cleansed, will only rob the child of God of happiness, and if ignored can lead to more serious sin. As the believer moves, then, through this corrupt world, let the death of Christ always be remembered, the Holy Spirit's power through the Word constantly applied, and God's centre of gathering kept pure".

The Wood Offering

The Origin

The Wood Offering is only mentioned twice in the Scriptures, and only in the Book of Nehemiah, as noted above. But although there is no direct reference to it in the Book of Leviticus it was nevertheless essential for the maintenance of the altar fire upon which the Levitical Offerings were burned. It had been distinctly commanded by Jehovah that this fire must never go out. It must never be put out nor be allowed, through negligence, to go out. "And the fire upon the altar shall be burning in it; it shall not be put out: and the priest shall burn wood on it every morning, and lay the burnt offering in order upon it; and he shall burn thereon the fat of the peace offerings ... The fire shall ever be burning upon the altar; it shall never go out" (Lev ch 6. vv 12-13).

There was no Wood Offering in the days before the captivity since the necessary wood was brought to the temple by the Nethinim. These were captives, prisoners of war, who had been allocated to the Levites to relieve them of the more menial tasks, and they were accordingly described as "hewers of wood and drawers of water" (Josh ch 9. vv 21-27). They were descendants of the Gibeonites but were now, literally, slaves to the Levites. After the exile however, many of the Nethinim apparently opted to remain in the land of their captivity when the Jews returned to their own land under Zerubbabel and Ezra. Only about six hundred Nethinim came back with the Jews and consequently the provision of the wood for the altar now became the responsibility of the Levites themselves, who were indeed, the original Temple servants (Ezra ch 2.v 58; ch 8. v20).

Adam Clarke sums this up, saying, "There does not appear to have been any wood-offering under the law. It was the business of the Nethinim to procure this; and hence they were called hewers of wood and drawers of water to the congregation. But it is very likely that after the captivity few Nethinim were found; for as such, who were the descendants of the Gibeonites, were considered only as slaves among the Israelites, they would doubtless find it as much, if not more, in their interest to abide in the land of their captivity, than to return with their former masters. As there were not enough of such persons to provide wood for the fires of the temple, the people now cast lots, not who should furnish the wood, but what class or district should furnish it at a particular time of the year, so that there might be a constant supply".

The Necessity

After a consideration of the Levitical Offerings the importance of the Wood Offering should be obvious. The fire of the altar must burn continually therefore a continual supply of wood was essential. Without it, sacrifice and offerings would cease. There could be no worship as in the Burnt Offerings and Meat Offerings, for both of these were burned on the altar. There could be no fellowship as in the Peace Offerings since these too were burned on the altar fire. There could be no atonement for the guilty since Sin Offerings and Trespass Offerings would not be possible. How absolutely necessary for the maintenance of Temple ritual was this apparently insignificant offering of wood. Such was the importance of the Wood Offering that the practice of bringing wood eventually assumed the character of a Feast or Festival. Josephus refers to this though it is never so called in Scripture, nor is it ever reckoned among the Feasts of the Jews, as are some other Festivals which are extra Scriptural. The wood which was brought, whether by individuals or by families or by districts, was first examined by the priests and then stored in a "wood room" or "wood chamber" until it was required for the altar.

The Lesson

The lessons for the believer today are relatively simple and very practical. There are matters which, to some, may appear insignificant but which are necessary if the fires of devotion and testimony are to be kept alive. We can all play our part, albeit perhaps humbly, in the maintenance of the life of the assembly.

There is, of course, the question of our presence at the gatherings of the saints. If this was to be neglected by all its members then soon there would be no collective worship, no assembly intercessions, and no evangelical witness. However apparently unimportant it may seem, yet my presence at the meetings for Remembrance, Prayer, Bible Reading and Gospel preaching is so necessary. We must therefore recognise this and rise to our responsibility to be present always if at all possible.

Then there is the matter of my prayers. Every assembly has need. There are sick and suffering saints, and maybe there are those who are straying. There are overseers, responsible brethren who carry a heavy burden in caring for the saints and they do need our help by our intercessions.

Again, there is my participation. No matter how small, every saint can offer some participation while gifted brethren carry the responsibility of using their gift in ministry. Saints need to be fed, to be encouraged, to be exhorted. Those who are gifted in such ministry must not sit back but contribute in a helpful way to the life of the assembly. By our presence, our prayers, and our participation we can all play our part in keeping the fire of worship and testimony alive.

The Privilege

Such services as have been mentioned are not burdensome chores, but privileges. Every assembly is a lampstand in its district. The light, like the altar fire must not be put out nor must it be allowed to go out through negligence. The reward? The purpose of such a light in the district is that Christ might be glorified. What a privilege it is that I may play a part in proclaiming the glory of Christ in my district. The Saviour has only His saints to proclaim on earth His power and His worth. There is nothing and no one else in the world to exalt and extol Him and it is therefore a great privilege indeed to be involved in testimony to Him. My contribution may be as humble as the bringing of wood to the altar, but it is appreciated by the Saviour, and one day, at the Judgment Seat, He will acknowledge this, and "every man shall have praise of God" (1 Cor ch 4. v 5).

Bibliography

BOYD, Dr John *The Levitical Offerings*. Fareham U.K. Precious Seed Publications 2009. First published as a series of articles in Precious Seed Magazine 1965-66.
An excellent treatment of the main Levitical Offerings with a helpful chapter also on the Drink Offering.

CALDWELL, John R. *Christ in the Levitical Offerings*. Glasgow. Pickering & Inglis. Undated.
This small volume is a sweet and scholarly treatise on the five principal Offerings. It has a value out of all proportion to its size.

CLARKE, Adam. *Leviticus*. Adam Clarke's Commentary. Grand Rapids MI. U.S.A. Baker Book House 1967. A one-volume edition edited by Ralph Earle.
Originally a six-volume work in an 18th Century style of writing but a very scholarly and consistently helpful commentary.

DARBY, J.N. *Synopsis of the Books of the Bible. Vol 1.* Kingston-on-Thames. Stow Hill Bible and Tract Depot. 1964.
As Mr Darby himself states in his Preface, this is not a commentary, not a verse-by-verse exposition. JND's writings are not the easiest to read but for those who study them patiently they are an invaluable mine of spiritual teaching and this volume is no exception.

JAMIESON, FAUSSET and BROWN. (JFB) *Commentary on Leviticus*. Grand Rapids Michigan. Wm. B. Erdmans Publishing Co. Reprint.
Originally published 1871, the JFB commentaries have long been highly appreciated. They are Evangelical, Critical, Experimental, and Practical, and give much help.

JUKES, Andrew *The Law of the Offerings*. London. Pickering & Inglis. Undated
Reckoned by many to be the classic work on the Levitical Offerings and a fine, readable introduction to the subject for any believer.

KINGSCOTE, R. F. *Christ as seen in the Offerings*. London. G. Morrish. Undated.
Notes of addresses given by the author in Park Street, London in the early days of the revival of assembly testimony in the 19th Century. A small volume of helpful meditations presenting, as the title indicates, Christ as seen in the Offerings.

MACKINTOSH, C. H. *Notes on the Book of Leviticus*. Neptune, New Jersey. 1972
First published in 1881 and six volumes later became known as "Notes on the Pentateuch" (Genesis, Exodus, Leviticus, Numbers, and two volumes on Deuteronomy). The 1972 Volume is the first Edition of the six books in one volume. More of a meditation than an exposition but rich in precious thoughts of the Person and Work of Christ as is characteristic of C. H. M.

NEWBERRY, Thomas. *Types of the Levitical Offerings*. Kilmarnock. John Ritchie Ltd. Third Edition. Undated
A concise consideration of the principal Offerings, by the Editor of the well-known Newberry Bible. Also added are brief comments on the Consecration of the Priests, the Day of Atonement, the Cleansing of the Leper and the Ashes of the Red Heifer. A small but profitable volume with much of Christ in it.

NEWTON, B.W. *Thoughts on Parts of Leviticus*. London. The Sovereign Grace Advent Testimony. First Edition 1852. Reprinted 1898.
A scholarly treatment of the early chapters of Leviticus with very helpful notes and comments on the Priesthood and Offerings. Christ exalting ministry.

POLLOCK, A. J. *The Tabernacle's Typical Teaching*. London. Pickering & Inglis. Undated.
A helpful little volume in the clear diction of A.J Pollock, dealing mainly with the Tabernacle in the Wilderness and its rich foreshadowings of Christ. There are however, several chapters on the Offerings, the Great Day of Atonement and the Feasts of Jehovah. Well worth having, and reading. An excellent introduction for younger believers coming to the subject for the first time.

SCOTT, Walter *The Tabernacle; its Structure, Vessels, Coverings, Sacrifices and Services*. Goodmayes, Essex. Undated
Written by a well-known and reliable writer, this volume deals mainly with the Tabernacle itself but has some thirty pages devoted to the Offerings. These are indeed only notes but they deal succinctly with the salient points of each Offering.

STUBBS, John J. *Numbers. What the Bible Teaches*. Kilmarnock. John Ritchie Ltd 2003.
This volume contains a most comprehensive, thorough, and in-depth consideration of the ordinance of the Red Heifer (Numbers 19), with which are associated some of the Levitical Offerings.

WHITE, Frank H. *Christ in the Tabernacle* London. S.W.Partridge 1905.
An excellent work on the Tabernacle in general, including, as its sub-title says, "some remarks on the Offerings". There is in fact, a chapter on each of the five principal Offerings, all most helpful. A valuable work, highly recommended.